The PEOPLE,
the PRESS,
& POLITICS

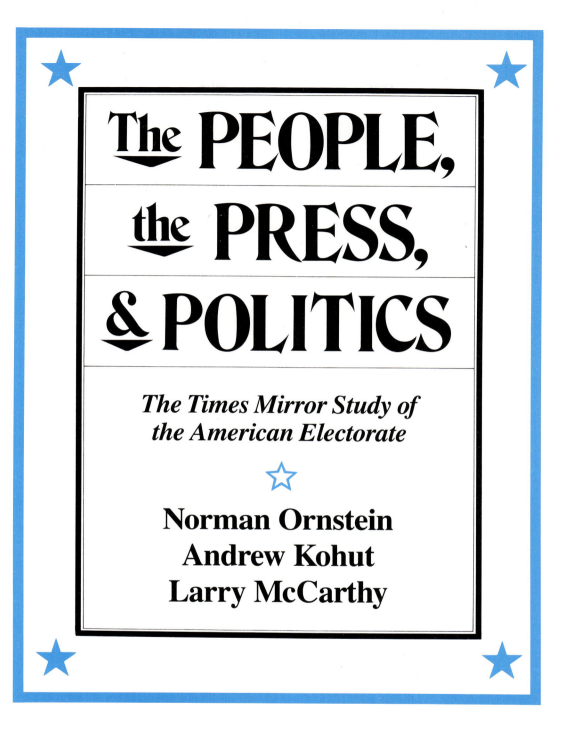

The PEOPLE, the PRESS, & POLITICS

The Times Mirror Study of the American Electorate

Norman Ornstein
Andrew Kohut
Larry McCarthy

Addison-Wesley Publishing Company, Inc.

Reading, Massachusetts ★ Menlo Park, California
New York ★ Don Mills, Ontario ★ Wokingham, England
Amsterdam ★ Bonn ★ Sydney ★ Singapore ★ Tokyo
Madrid   San Juan

Cover design by Copenhaver Cumpston

ABCDEFGHIJ-DO-898
First printing, January 1988

FOREWORD

Three years ago, Times Mirror embarked upon an ambitious program to learn more about what Americans think about the news media. We commissioned The Gallup Organization to conduct a series of surveys to gauge public attitudes on a range of press issues.

Today, with a presidential election approaching, we have expanded the focus of this "The People & the Press" program to address a broader issue—the growing imprecision in the very language of politics and public opinion.

Working with The Gallup Organization and its president, Andrew Kohut, and with Dr. Norman Ornstein of the American Enterprise Institute, we have conducted a study that identifies the beliefs and behaviors that underlie political labels and drive political action.

We have two hopes for this study. We hope it will help all of us in the news media to report more precisely about political issues, and we hope it will enable Americans to make more informed choices in 1988 and beyond.

Robert F. Erburu

ROBERT F. ERBURU
Chairman and Chief Executive Officer
Times Mirror

INTRODUCTION

On the basis of the most exhaustive study of the American electorate ever undertaken, we suggest an entirely new way of looking at—and reporting on—American politics.

We will show that the conventional way of defining our politics—in terms such as liberal and conservative, Republican, Democrat and independent—bears little relation to the true, diverse nature of the electorate.

We will divide that electorate into distinct, new constituencies and identify the fundamental outlooks on life and major institutions that animate virtually all American political behavior.

We will demonstrate that:
- the winning coalition built by Ronald Reagan in 1980 and 1984 will be enormously difficult for the Republican nominee to hold in 1988;
- social justice, rather than economic satisfaction, will probably be the most important single issue in 1988;
- the largest constituency of the Democratic Party is dying and not being replaced;
- two-thirds of the most sophisticated and influential Republicans and Democrats hold a favorable view of Mikhail Gorbachev;

- no amount of economic progress turns black Americans into Republicans;
- our traditional view of the parties—Republicans are free enterprise-oriented, affluent and conservative, while Democrats are peace-oriented, social reformers and liberals—holds true for only one-third of the population;
- Americans under 30 have far more faith in government and big business than do their elders.

As these highlights of the study suggest, much conventional wisdom about American politics must now be discarded. But what is most important about this study is the unprecedented sweep and intimacy it brings to its portrayal of the American electorate.

To our colleagues in journalism, to those in the political world who seek to lead a remarkable people and most of all to the self-governing American citizens themselves who are the endlessly fascinating subject of this study, Times Mirror respectfully submits *The People, the Press & Politics.*

TABLE OF CONTENTS

PRINCIPAL
FINDINGS

1

1. *There are 11 distinct groups in the American electorate—10 that vote in varying degrees, and one that does not vote at all.* How Americans vote is a much more complex process than previously defined. There have been many attempts to analyze political attitudes in this country. Some analysts have focused on party as the key factor, while others stress ideology, issues or generation. But the Times Mirror study conducted by The Gallup Organization, based on 4,244 exhaustive, in-person interviews, reveals far more complexity and many more voting factors than have previously been quantified and analyzed.

2. *In 1987, the conventional labels of "liberal" and "conservative" are about as relevant as the words "Whig" and "Federalist."* While Americans may respond to the *terms* "liberal" and "conservative," these expressions have not only lost much of their traditional meaning, they do not even remotely come close to defining the nature of American public opinion. We find nine basic values and orientations that both drive— and divide—Americans:
  - *Religious Faith*—Belief in God
  - *Tolerance*—Belief in freedom for those who don't share one's values
  - *Social Justice*—Belief in the government's obligation to ensure social justice and social welfare

  - *Militant Anti-Communism*—Belief in a strong, aggressive military defense to halt communism
  - *Alienation*—Belief that the American system does not work for oneself
  - *American Exceptionalism*—Belief that there are no limits to what America can do
  - *Financial Pressure*—Belief about one's financial status
  - *Attitudes toward Government*—Belief about the proper role and effectiveness of government
  - *Attitudes toward Business Corporations*—Belief about the goals and effectiveness of business corporations

These basic values and orientations, whatever positions the individuals may hold, define American political attitudes much more clearly than the commonly used concepts of "liberal" and "conservative."

3. *The Republican Party has two distinct groups*: the *Enterprisers*, whose more traditional form of Republicanism is driven by free enterprise economic concerns, and the *Moralists*, an equally large, less affluent and more populist group driven by moral issues and Militant Anti-Communism.

4. *The Democratic Party has four blocs, partially defined by generation and class, and divided on the values of Tolerance and Militant Anti-Communism. New Dealers,* the largest group, are older, more traditional, less tolerant and more anti-communist. *Sixties Democrats* are largely in their thirties and forties, upper-middle class, tolerant and driven by the issues of peace and social justice. The *Partisan Poor* are disproportionately black, financially pressured, highly politicized and have an extraordinary faith in the Democratic Party. The *Passive Poor* are also low income, but are less politicized and much less critical of American institutions and their own status in life than are the Partisan Poor.

5. *A full 11 percent of American adults are totally uninvolved in public affairs and politics. Bystanders* have almost no interest in politics, no history of voting and no inclination to participate in the future. Demographically, Bystanders are young, white and poorly educated.

6. *There are four remaining independent groups in the electorate—two that lean Republican and two Democratic.* The two Republican-leaning groups are equal in size, but differ dramatically from one another in their outlook on life and politics. *Upbeats* are young, optimistic, strong believers in American Exceptionalism and appear to be an important legacy of the Reagan presidency. *Disaffecteds* are the reverse—middle-aged, pessimistic and distrustful of business and government alike. The Democratic-leaning groups also differ widely from one another. *Seculars* are affluent, well-informed, tolerant and peace-oriented—and defined largely by their lack of religious beliefs. *Followers* are poor, young and uninformed. They show little faith in America, but are surprisingly uncritical of its institutions.

7. *In national politics, it is a virtual toss-up between the Republicans and the Democrats.* We see no evidence of a Republican realignment or an emerging Republican majority. At the most basic level, our survey shows the Democrats maintaining their advantage in party identification. Among likely voters, 41 percent of the public fit in core Democratic Party categories and 30 percent in core Republican Party categories.

The balance narrows when we take into account voters that lean toward one party or the other; 16 percent of voters lean Republican; 13 percent Democratic. But the 54 percent to 46 percent Democratic edge narrows still further when we factor in probable voter turnout.

Contrary to conventional wisdom, it's not just the Democrats who have a turnout problem. A low voter turnout does not simply hurt the Democrats and help the Republicans. The turnout problem for the Republicans is in the leaning groups we call Upbeats and Disaffecteds. The Democrats' turnout problem is more serious because they not only have to worry about turning out their two leaning groups, but the party has continual problems turning out its four core groups. The result will probably be a 1988 presidential race that is very close.

8. *Despite its improved standing after 1984, the Democratic Party continues to be perceived as having a competence and management problem, and a problem selecting good candidates—*an image that exists among Democrats and non-Democrats alike. Among Democratic groups, Seculars and '60s Democrats are especially suspicious of their own candidates.

9. *The potential Republican majority built by Ronald Reagan is in four diverse parts and could easily crumble after his term.* Two of the parts are ideological and policy-driven (Enterprisers and Moralists), while the others are moved less by ideas than by personalities (Disaffecteds) and symbolic themes (Upbeats).

10. *The Reagan record is both the good news and the bad news for the Republican Party.* Responses to the famous Reagan question, "Are you better off now than you were five years ago?," continue to break in favor of Republicans among most voting groups. But when asked about the future of the country, Americans display a growing lack of confidence, especially in light of the Iran-Contra affair. This lack of confidence reduces the Republicans' ability to run on the Reagan record.

11. *Increased by the evangelical movement, the GOP's non-establishment wing—the Moralists—is likely to be equal in strength in the 1988 primaries to the traditional Republican wing—the Enterprisers.* In fact, George Bush's early lead in the polls is due to his high level of support among Moralists, not Enterprisers. Even though the Enterprisers are assumed to be Bush's natural constituency, his strength among this group fails to match his support among Moralists.

12. *Republicans have done a better job than Democrats in luring previously independent voters.* The Democrats' overall edge in numbers is due largely to their parents—more people are born Democrat than Republican. But the GOP has won over more of those people who have no roots in either party, giving them hope that in the long run they can finally achieve their Holy Grail of being the majority party.

"A full 11 percent of American adults are totally uninvolved in public affairs and politics."

13. *The Democratic Party can no longer claim to be the party of the young.* Less than a decade ago, people under 30 were grouped with minorities and union members as a natural constituency for the Democratic Party. But the two parties are now virtually even among the young, with men tilting Republican and women remaining Democratic.

14. *Religion plays an important—but surprising—role in American politics, both in its presence and absence in crucial voting blocs.* Religion in politics goes far beyond the presidential candidacies of the Revs. Robertson and Jackson. Belief in God—or the lack of such belief—is a key American value. Deep religious faith helps define several American voter groups. But contrary to conventional wisdom, deep religious faith (or evangelicalism, or "born-again" Christianity) is not simply a phenomenon of the political right. It is there on the right, among the Moralists. But it is also a major factor on the other side of the political spectrum. Three solidly Democratic groups—the New Dealers, '60s Democrats and Partisan Poor—express deep religious beliefs equal to those of the Moralists. The large number of black evangelicals is a major reason for the depth of religious feeling among these Democratic groups.

Just as significant, one of the most important voting groups, a full nine percent of the electorate, is *defined by its lack of religion.* Seculars tend to be white, well educated and middle-aged, and are concentrated on both coasts.

15. *The greatest failure of the Democratic Party has been its inability to attract the Seculars* —a large bloc of voters who look like Democrats, think like Democrats, but remain outside the party. The Seculars have the resources and political sophistication to energize the party and to make the difference in a close election.

16. *Black voters are overwhelmingly Democratic, but they are not monolithic in their beliefs.* Like whites, blacks divide on Tolerance, Militant Anti-Communism and, most importantly, belief in America's ability to deal with its problems. The single largest group of black Americans (26 percent) are Partisan Poor, but substantial numbers of blacks are New Dealers, '60s Democrats, Passive Poor and Followers.

- Poor blacks are more politicized than poor whites.
- Blacks do not desert the Democratic Party as they move up the socioeconomic ladder—many become '60s Democrats, while others retain the political attitudes of the poor.

17. *After giving Ronald Reagan significant support in 1980 and 1984, core Democratic groups returned in large numbers to their party in the 1986 congressional elections, but when questioned about 1988, they once again show their tendency to defect.* Only the Partisan Poor support Democratic presidential candidates at the same rate core Republican groups support GOP candidates.

18. *Social Justice—whether you believe government should help the disadvantaged and guarantee equality—looms larger than any other single value in 1988.* Social Justice is a crucial factor to a large number of voters, plus it is the one value that unifies the Democratic Party throughout its various voting groups—and that distinguishes it from the Republicans.

19. *Tolerance—one's openness to different views and lifestyles—is a value that divides the cores of both parties, but it is especially divisive for the Democrats.*

20. *Militant Anti-Communism—aggressive anti-communism coupled with enthnocentrism (the belief that America and its people are superior to others)—is a value that divides the generations and the sexes, and it more often divides the Democratic Party than the Republicans.*

21. *American Exceptionalism—having a positive, "can do" attitude about the United States—* appears to be an important political value brought into focus by Ronald Reagan. Views on American Exceptionalism distinguish people with a Republican orientation from those with a Democratic orientation, even when parental links to the party are taken into account.

22. *Attitudes toward Government, Attitudes toward Business Corporations, Alienation and Financial Pressure—are important political values that help structure the electorate;* but at this point, they do not appear to be playing an important role in voter thinking about 1988.

"Blacks do not desert the Democratic Party as they move up the socioeconomic ladder..."

23. *The political values of the two core Republican groups clash on issues relating to Tolerance and the use of government to achieve Social Justice.* Moralists generally condemn lifestyles and points of view that are outside of a narrowly defined mainstream of American life. But Moralists are not opposed to social spending provided it is not targeted at minorities. In contrast, Enterprisers are much more tolerant in their views, but their fiscal conservatism drives them to oppose nearly all forms of social spending. Potentially divisive issues between these two GOP groups are AIDS, abortion and federal programs for the middle class.

24. *Militant Anti-Communism does not seem likely to divide the Democratic Party in 1988, as it did in the Vietnam Era.* There is no major foreign policy issue on the horizon that can bring to a flashpoint this major value difference within the party.

25. *The attitudinal groups join together in unusual coalitions that defy party lines:*

- Enterprisers, Seculars and '60s Democrats tend to share issue positions that are dependent upon political sophistication.
- Moralists, New Dealers and Passive Poor share views on censorship.
- The Partisan Poor, Passive Poor and '60s Democrats share views on government spending.
- Moralists, New Dealers, Passive Poor and Disaffecteds often express the same opinion on defense and foreign policy matters.

26. *America has more than just one generation gap.* The classic generation gap—young vs. old—does exist, but with two separate themes: 1) those over 45 years of age (pre-World War II) are much more likely to express strong anti-communist feelings than those who are under 45 (post-World War II); and 2) those under 30 years of age have much more basic faith in American institutions, such as business and government, than do their elders.

The survey also found that there are four voting blocs that have clear generational colorings—Upbeats (predominantly under 30); Seculars and '60s Democrats (30 to 44); and New Dealers (50 plus)—legacies, respectively, of Reagan, Kennedy and FDR.

Young voters, however, are not a monolithic bloc. The presumed existence of a "yuppie" vote is shattered by our findings. Voters who fit that profile—under 40, college-educated, relatively affluent—can be found in at least four diverse groups, from Enterprisers on the Republican side to the '60s Democrats on the Democratic side.

27. *Voters who rely on newspapers rather than television for information on national affairs are more sophisticated and, on balance, more Republican than the nation as a whole.* Newspaper readers are more tolerant, less alienated, yet less religious and less in favor of social welfarism.

28. *Political advertising has its greatest impact on less sophisticated voters in both the Democratic and Republican camps*—Moralists on the Republican side and all Democrats except '60s Democrats are especially likely to rely on advertising to get an idea of what candidates are like.

THE ROAD TO THE TYPOLOGY

2

Americans have used the same basic political labels—Democrats, Republicans, liberals, conservatives, populists—for longer than most people can remember. As time has passed, more labels have evolved—libertarians, the New Right, the Old Left. Most recently, we have added such demographic acronyms as "yuppies," "DINKs" and "POSSLQs" (couples with *D*ouble *I*ncome, *N*o *K*ids and *P*ersons of the *O*pposite *S*ex *S*haring *L*iving *Q*uarters).

Political scientists call labels such as these "typologies," because members of the respective groups presumably share a common set of political beliefs. But current political typologies fail to describe the American electorate with sufficient precision to determine why voters choose a given political candidate. And they fail to explain why shifting coalitions of the public come together on some issues and divide on others.

Although political party affiliation remains the single best indicator of voters' candidate preferences as well as the best individual measure of political behavior, the American political landscape is a minefield of contradictions. For the past 20 years, the Democratic Party has enjoyed a large advantage in the number of Americans who profess political allegiance to its standard. Yet in those same 20 years, Democrats have lost four out of five presidential elections—three by landslides.

As many elections and public opinion surveys have shown, party identification *alone* offers an insufficient typology of the American electorate. But it remains an important ingredient in developing a new voter typology, because in 1987, party identification continues to be the focus of organized politics in America.

Another commonly used method of political classification is by ideology. Most analysts refer to conservatives, moderates and liberals. Some add color and account for complexity with terms such as "extra-chromosome conservatives" and "knee-jerk liberals." But no matter what the terminology, contradictions abound. One may simultaneously be a fiscal conservative and hold liberal views on the environment. Someone else might be very liberal on social issues, but still opposed to abortion. And opinion surveys regularly show that most Americans simultaneously favor a reduction in overall government spending and an increase in spending for a broad array of specific programs.

Typologies developed from generational subgroups are the new fashion in classifying the electorate. Some demographically defined political types, such as "yuppies," have been casually assumed to share a common set of political values. Other demographic typologies reflect groups that share traditional characteristics with a given electoral pattern—blacks, labor union members, the affluent, business leaders, etc.

Political typologies based on social-demographic characteristics alone are inadequate indicators of voter attitudes, and they do a poor job of predicting voter behavior.

A NEW POLITICAL TYPOLOGY
In developing a new political typology, it was essential for us to meet several goals. At a minimum, the typology must do a better job than traditional typologies in measuring voter preferences. The new typology should show how personal attitudes shape voters' political behavior and influence their choice of candidates for political office. To meet these goals, the new typology would have to be able to classify Americans into mutually exclusive categories. It was our view that we could best achieve these aims by combining two types of indicators: basic social and political values, and political and ideological self-identifications.

To begin the process, we reviewed major academic studies and survey data back to the 1960s. From these sources, we summarized these 21 general beliefs, values, political outlooks and personal orientations that have been shown to influence voter behavior:

I. Psychological
   1. Alienation
   2. Individualism
II. Government/Political
   3. Political participation
   4. Size and power of government
   5. Effectiveness of government
   6. Anti-elitism
   7. Limits to growth/power
   8. Egalitarianism
   9. Welfarism
   10. Pragmatism
III. Foreign Affairs
   11. Militarism
   12. Ethnocentrism/Patriotism
   13. Isolationism
   14. Anti-Communism
IV. Social/Moral
   15. Racial attitudes
   16. Religious faith
   17. Tolerance/Libertarianism/Freedom of expression
   18. Labor consciousness
   19. Class consciousness
V. Economic/Financial
   20. Beliefs about business
   21. Personal financial satisfaction

We tested these 21 items in 72 questions on our survey. As much as one-quarter of each interview was spent measuring these basic values and orientations of American politics.

To determine the relative strength of these 21 elements in the electorate, we employed a technique called "factor analysis."

Factor analysis is a mathematical tool that examines the relationships among responses to many questions collectively, rather than examining each response individually. The goal of factor analysis is to identify patterns of response that give insight into how people organize their thinking, and why people respond as they do to a wide range of questions.

Factor analysis holds the key to understanding the underlying organization of public opinion on a vast range of issues. It can be used to distill the complexity of respondents' answers to a large set of questions into a relatively small set of descriptive, efficient and highly predictive predispositions or factors.

Factor analysis has a second advantage. In effect, it allows the public to speak for itself about these underlying dimensions of opinion. Rather than assuming, a priori, what predispositions constitute the mindset of Americans, factor analysis looks inside the data and provides a statistical basis for identifying what they really are.

Using factor analysis, we found *nine* basic values and personal orientations that, taken together, provide the motivation for virtually all political behavior in America. They can be thought of as the themes in people's answers. The nine elements are divided between *three personal orientations* and *six basic value systems*. They are fully described in Appendix A and summarized below:

PERSONAL ORIENTATIONS

Religious Faith is a measure of belief in God. Two key demographic groups—women and blacks—are much more religious than average. Politically active people also tend to be more religious than average. But one highly political group is best defined by its lack of religion. Religious faith was determined by responses to several agree/disagree questions. Below are examples of the agree/disagree questions we used to measure this orientation:

> *Even today miracles are performed by the power of God.*
> *I am sometimes very conscious of the presence of God.*
> *Prayer is an important part of my daily life.*
> *We will all be called before God on Judgment Day to answer for our sins.*

Alienation represents the degree of powerlessness, hopelessness and the lack of trust in government people feel. Non-voters are more likely to be alienated. Key questions were:

> *People like me don't have any say about what the government does.*
> *Generally speaking, elected officials in Washington lose touch with the people pretty quickly.*
> *It is time for Washington politicians to step aside and make room for new leaders.*

Financial Pressure is the degree of financial concern felt by the respondents. This factor is determined to a significant degree by income itself, but it goes beyond the objective measure of dollars and cents to reflect self-perception of one's financial health.

> *I often don't have enough money to make ends meet.*
> *Money is one of my most important concerns.*
> *I'm pretty well satisfied with the way things are going for me financially.*

BASIC VALUE SYSTEMS

Tolerance/Intolerance gauges the degree to which people value civil liberties and free speech, and the extent to which they accept others who choose a different lifestyle. This factor also encompasses feelings about traditional social values and the role of women in society.

> *Books that contain dangerous ideas should be banned from public school libraries.*
> *School boards ought to have the right to fire teachers who are known homosexuals.*
> *Women should return to their traditional role in society.*
> *AIDS might be God's punishment for immoral sexual behavior.*
> *I think it's all right for blacks and whites to date each other.*

Social Justice measures beliefs about welfarism, social class standing and the role of government in providing for the needy.

> *The government should guarantee every citizen enough to eat and a place to sleep.*
> *The government should help more needy people even if it means going deeper into debt.*
> *We should make every possible effort to improve the position of blacks and other minorities, even if it means giving them preferential treatment.*

"Women and blacks are much more religious than average."

Militant Anti-Communism reflects perceptions about the threat of communism, militarism, the use of force to further American interests and ethnocentrism (the belief that America and her people are superior to others).

> *Communists are responsible for a lot of the unrest in the United States today.*
> *Communist countries are all alike.*
> *The best way to ensure peace is through military strength.*
> *American lives are worth more than the lives of people in other countries.*

Attitudes toward Government measures beliefs about the size and effectiveness of government.

> *When something is run by the government, it is usually inefficient and wasteful.*
> *The federal government controls too much of our daily lives.*
> *Government regulation of business usually does more harm than good.*

American Exceptionalism represents a belief in America that combines love of country with a view that the United States has a boundless ability to solve its problems.

> *I don't believe that there are any real limits to growth in this country today.*
> *As Americans, we can always find a way to solve our problems and get what we want.*
> *I am very patriotic.*
> *The strength of this country today is mostly based on the success of American business.*

Attitudes toward Business Corporations measures beliefs about the power and influence of American "big business."

> *There is too much power concentrated in the hands of a few big companies.*
> *Business corporations earn too much profit.*
> *Business corporations generally strike a fair balance between making profits and serving the public interest.*

MEASURING SELF-IDENTIFICATION

In addition to looking at how basic predispositions relate to public opinion, we also examined how Americans self-identify themselves politically. On a 1-10 scale, people were asked the extent to which they self-identify with 16 terms. It is important to note that although people *say*

these terms describe them, the overall pattern of their responses may contradict their self-identification. The results are fully described in Appendix B, but here is a brief summary.

Americans strongly identified (8-10 on the scale) with these terms by the following percentages:

Anti-Communist	70%
A religious person	49%
A supporter of the civil rights movement	47%
A supporter of the peace movement	46%
An environmentalist	39%
A supporter of the anti-abortion movement	32%
A Democrat	31%
A supporter of the women's movement	29%
A supporter of business interests	28%
A conservative	27%
A supporter of the National Rifle Association	27%
A union supporter	27%
Pro-Israel	25%
A Republican	20%
A liberal	19%
A supporter of the gay rights movement	8%

CREATING THE TYPOLOGY

To take the next step—creating a new and more useful voter typology—we needed to know how well these nine basic values and orientations and various measures of self-identification relate to modern politics. More specifically, we also needed to know whether the values and orientations *or* the self-identifications were the more useful predictors of voter behavior.

A statistical correlation of these elements known as "regression analysis" has led us to the following conclusions:

> *1. Although party does not correlate highly with opinions on most issues, it remains important to the way people organize their*

political choices. Any typology that deals with politics would fail to measure an important basic element if party identification were not represented.

2. *The nine basic values and orientations that emerge from our research relate strongly to public attitudes on a wide range of issues. When combined with party identification, they also improve our understanding of the respondents' political choices.*

3. *Ideological self-identification, whether one considers oneself a liberal or a conservative, does not play an important role for most Americans. It is a poor surrogate for one's basic political values.*

4. *Self-identification with issue positions and movements is highly correlated with the nine basic values. However, in the end, basic values appear to be a more sound analytical tool than self-identification because values are more broadly based and less tied to contemporary politics.*

The Times Mirror voter typology is primarily constructed by classifying people according to their nine basic values and orientations, and party affiliation. The only other element taken into account is the individual's interest and participation in politics and public affairs. Respondents are classified into three political involvement groups—high, average and low—based on their voting history and interest in public affairs. The low involvement group, 11 percent of the population, shows virtually no interest in politics, has no history of past voting and shows no inclination to vote in the future.

Utilizing a statistical technique called "cluster analysis" (which classifies the 4,244 respondents into the most homogeneous and meaningful statistical groups possible, based on all the variables described above), we were able at last to identify 10 distinct groups of American voters and one group of voting-age people who have no interest or involvement in politics at all.

Two groups are solidly Republican, four are Democratic and five are independent (although two of the independent groups lean Republican and two lean Democratic).

PROFILES

3

ENTERPRISE REPUBLICANS (*"Enterprisers"*)

10% ADULT POPULATION
16% LIKELY ELECTORATE

SUMMARY: Affluent, educated, 99% white, this group forms one of the two bedrocks of the Republican Party. As the name implies, Enterprisers are pro-business and anti-government. But what may surprise some is their tolerance and moderation on questions of personal freedom.

WHO THEY ARE: 60% male, married, Northern European ancestry, suburban.

KEY ATTITUDES: Top concern is budget deficit, but overwhelmingly disapprove of tax increases to cut deficit. Oppose increased spending for health care, aid to homeless and programs for the elderly. Oppose more restrictions on abortion and quarantine for AIDS patients. Support "Star Wars" and aid to the Contras.

LIFESTYLE NOTE: Group most likely to belong to a fraternal or civic organization; enjoy classical music.

VOTING LIKELIHOOD: High

PAST VOTE: '86 Congressional—89% Republican
'84 Presidential—96% Reagan
'80 Presidential—93% Reagan

INFORMATION LEVEL: Very high

HEROES: Ronald Reagan, Lee Iacocca

KEY EVENTS: Vietnam, the Reagan presidency

MORAL REPUBLICANS (*"Moralists"*)

11% ADULT POPULATION
14% LIKELY ELECTORATE

SUMMARY: Middle-aged, middle income, with a heavy concentration of Southerners, this group forms the second bedrock of the Republican Party. Moralists hold strong and very conservative views on social and foreign policy.

WHO THEY ARE: 94% white, live in suburbs, small cities and rural areas, regular church-goers with a large number of "born-again" Christians.

KEY ATTITUDES: Strongly anti-abortion, pro-school prayer, favor death penalty and quarantine on AIDS patients, strongly anti-communist, pro-defense, favor social spending except when it is targeted to minorities. Deficit and unemployment cited as top concerns.

VOTING LIKELIHOOD: High

PAST VOTE: '86 Congressional—95% Republican
'84 Presidential—97% Reagan
'80 Presidential—92% Reagan

INFORMATION LEVEL: Average

HEROES: Ronald Reagan, Billy Graham

KEY EVENTS: Vietnam, the Reagan presidency

UPBEATS

9% ADULT POPULATION
9% LIKELY ELECTORATE

SUMMARY: Young, optimistic and strong believers in America, this group leans solidly to the GOP. Unlike most groups (especially Republican-leaning groups), the Upbeats are *not* critical of the government's role in society.

WHO THEY ARE: Middle income, little or no college, 94% white, under 40, strongly pro-Reagan.

KEY ATTITUDES: Identify the deficit and economic concerns as top problems, give moderate support to "Star Wars," but oppose Contra aid and fear it will lead to military involvement.

LIFESTYLE NOTE: Enjoy rock 'n' roll, have highest readership of romance novels.

VOTING LIKELIHOOD: Average

PAST VOTE: '86 Congressional—64% Republican
'84 Presidential—86% Reagan
'80 Presidential—78% Reagan

INFORMATION LEVEL: Average

HEROES: Ronald Reagan, Lee Iacocca, John F. Kennedy

KEY EVENTS: Vietnam, the Reagan presidency

DISAFFECTEDS

9% ADULT POPULATION
7% LIKELY ELECTORATE

SUMMARY: Alienated, pessimistic, skeptical of both big government and big business, this group leans Republican, but many of its members have historic ties to Democratic Party.

WHO THEY ARE: Middle-aged, middle income, slightly more male than average, Disaffecteds live in higher numbers in the Midwest. Disaffecteds say they feel significant personal financial pressure.

KEY ATTITUDES: Strongly anti-government and anti-business, but pro-military, Disaffecteds strongly support capital punishment and oppose gun control. They are divided on abortion. Generally support social spending unless specifically targeted to minorities. Unemployment and budget deficit are top concerns.

LIFESTYLE NOTE: Most Disaffecteds say Country and Western is their favorite music. Group with the highest number of hunters.

VOTING LIKELIHOOD: Slightly below average

PAST VOTE: '86 Congressional—57% Republican
'84 Presidential—81% Reagan
'80 Presidential—69% Reagan

INFORMATION LEVEL: Average

HEROES: None

KEY EVENTS: Vietnam, Watergate

BYSTANDERS

11% ADULT POPULATION
0% LIKELY ELECTORATE

SUMMARY: Young, poorly educated and marked by an almost total lack of interest in current affairs, Bystanders are just that—non-participants in American democracy.

WHO THEY ARE: Bystanders tend to be under 30, 82% white, 13% black, with a substantial number of unmarried individuals. When asked which party they prefer, Bystanders lean Democratic 34%-29%.

KEY ATTITUDES: This is the only group that says they do not care who is elected president in 1988—57% hold this view. To the extent they hold positions on issues, Bystanders tend to hold fairly conventional views. Their top concerns are unemployment, poverty and the threat of nuclear war.

LIFESTYLE NOTE: For many Bystanders, their favorite activity is going to clubs and discos.

VOTING LIKELIHOOD: Close to zero

PAST VOTE: —

INFORMATION LEVEL: Low

HEROES: John F. Kennedy

KEY EVENTS: Vietnam, the Reagan presidency

FOLLOWERS

7% ADULT POPULATION
4% LIKELY ELECTORATE

SUMMARY: With a very limited interest in politics, this group has little faith in America, but is surprisingly uncritical of both government and business. While they lean to the Democratic Party, Followers are very persuadable and unpredictable.

WHO THEY ARE: Young, poorly educated, blue-collar, Eastern and Southern, little religious commitment, 18% hispanic, 25% black (most of whom are under 30).

KEY ATTITUDES: Oppose "Star Wars" and favor increased spending to reduce unemployment. At the national midpoint on almost all other issues. While this group leans Democratic, it's divided on Reagan approval. Ted Kennedy receives strong support from this group.

LIFESTYLE NOTE: Of all the groups, Followers are the least likely to exercise regularly or read for pleasure.

VOTING LIKELIHOOD: Low

PAST VOTE: '86 Congressional—65% Democratic
'84 Presidential—54% Reagan
'80 Presidential—40% Reagan

INFORMATION LEVEL: Very Low

HEROES: John F. Kennedy

KEY EVENTS: Vietnam

SECULARS

8% ADULT POPULATION
9% LIKELY ELECTORATE

SUMMARY: The only group in America that professes no religious belief. This well-educated, white, middle-age group combines a strong commitment to personal freedom, moderate beliefs on social questions and a very low level of anti-communism. Despite their views, only a minority of Seculars think of themselves as Democrats and their political participation does not match their high level of knowledge and sophistication.

WHO THEY ARE: Heavily concentrated on the East and West coasts, professional, 11% Jewish.

KEY ATTITUDES: Favor cuts in military spending, oppose "Star Wars," school prayer, anti-abortion legislation, relaxing environmental controls. Top concern is budget deficit. On social spending, Seculars differ from core Democratic groups in opposing increased aid for minorities and farmers.

LIFESTYLE NOTE: Nearly one-half regularly attend theater, ballet or classical music concerts.

VOTING LIKELIHOOD: Slightly above average

PAST VOTE: '86 Congressional—72% Democratic
'84 Presidential —34% Reagan
'80 Presidential —29% Reagan

INFORMATION LEVEL: Very high

HEROES: Martin Luther King, Jr., John F. Kennedy, Franklin Delano Roosevelt

KEY EVENTS: Vietnam, Watergate

'60s DEMOCRATS

8% ADULT POPULATION
11% LIKELY ELECTORATE

SUMMARY: This upper-middle-class, heavily female (60%) group of mainstream Democrats has a strong commitment to social justice and a very low militancy level. They strongly identify with the peace, civil rights and environmental movements that grew out of the 1960s. They combine church-going and religious beliefs with a very high degree of tolerance for views and lifestyles they do not share.

WHO THEY ARE: Well-educated, married women with children, 16% black (most of whom are college educated).

KEY ATTITUDES: Favor increased spending on programs for minorities and most other forms of social spending. Strong opposition to "Star Wars." Feel U.S. is too suspicious of the Soviet Union. Although '60s Democrats support the Democratic agenda, they harbor doubts about some of the candidates the party nominates.

LIFESTYLE NOTE: Heavy readers, exercise regularly, work with youth groups.

VOTING LIKELIHOOD: High

PAST VOTE: '86 Congressional—85% Democratic
'84 Presidential—25% Reagan
'80 Presidential—18% Reagan

INFORMATION LEVEL: Very high

HEROES: Martin Luther King, Jr., John F. Kennedy

KEY EVENTS: Vietnam, civil rights movement, '60s assassinations

NEW DEAL DEMOCRATS ("*New Dealers*")

11% ADULT POPULATION
15% LIKELY ELECTORATE

SUMMARY: The roots of this aging group of traditional Democrats can be found in the New Deal Democratic coalition. Blue-collar, union members, moderate income with little financial pressure, religious, intolerant on questions of personal freedom, yet favor many social spending measures.

WHO THEY ARE: Older (66% over 50), 29% Catholic, less likely to live in the West.

KEY ATTITUDES: The largest group of Democrats with significant defections to Reagan in '84, they came back to the Democratic Party in 1986. Favor most social spending except when specifically targeted to minorities. Favor more restrictions on abortions, school prayer, protectionism and "Star Wars." Less concerned about the environment.

LIFESTYLE NOTE: Heavy television viewers, especially game shows, nighttime soaps and religious shows. Prefer Country and Western music.

VOTING LIKELIHOOD: High

PAST VOTE: '86 Congressional—92% Democratic
'84 Presidential—30% Reagan
'80 Presidential—21% Reagan

INFORMATION LEVEL: Average

HEROES: Franklin Delano Roosevelt,
John F. Kennedy

KEY EVENTS: The Depression, the New Deal

THE PASSIVE POOR

**7% ADULT POPULATION
6% LIKELY ELECTORATE**

SUMMARY: Older and poor, this solidly Democratic group has a strong faith in America and is uncritical of its institutions and leadership. Committed to social justice, the Passive Poor are also moderately anti-communist.

WHO THEY ARE: Less well-educated, Southern, 31% black, poor, but feel only moderate financial pressure.

KEY ATTITUDES: Favor all forms of increased social spending, more supportive of tax increases than any other group. Favor "Star Wars" and oppose cuts in defense spending. Moderately anti-abortion. Favor relaxing environmental standards for economic growth.

LIFESTYLE NOTE: Heavy television viewers.

VOTING LIKELIHOOD: Below average

PAST VOTE: '86 Congressional—83% Democratic
'84 Presidential—31% Reagan
'80 Presidential—21% Reagan

"The Passive Poor…(have) a strong faith in America and are uncritical of its institutions and leadership."

INFORMATION LEVEL: Low

HEROES: John F. Kennedy, Franklin Delano Roosevelt, Martin Luther King, Jr., Ted Kennedy

KEY EVENTS: Vietnam, '60s assassinations, the Depression

THE PARTISAN POOR

**9% ADULT POPULATION
9% LIKELY ELECTORATE**

SUMMARY: The most firmly Democratic group in the country—very low income, feel very high financial pressure. The Partisan Poor are very concerned with social justice issues and have a strong faith that the Democratic Party can achieve the social changes they want to see.

WHO THEY ARE: 37% black, low income, Southern, urban, poorly educated.

KEY ATTITUDES: Strong advocates of all social spending, but oppose tax increases. Favor death penalty, school prayer amendment, but divided on abortion. Unemployment top issue. Little concern for budget deficit, but favor cutting defense spending.

LIFESTYLE NOTE: Heavy television viewers, light readers.

VOTING LIKELIHOOD: Slightly above average

PAST VOTE: '86 Congressional—95% Democratic
'84 Presidential—19% Reagan
'80 Presidential—16% Reagan

INFORMATION LEVEL: Low

HEROES: John F. Kennedy, Martin Luther King, Jr., Franklin Delano Roosevelt, Ted Kennedy

KEY EVENTS: JFK presidency, '60s assassinations, civil rights movement

THE TYPOLOGY GROUPS:
HOW THEY VOTE

4

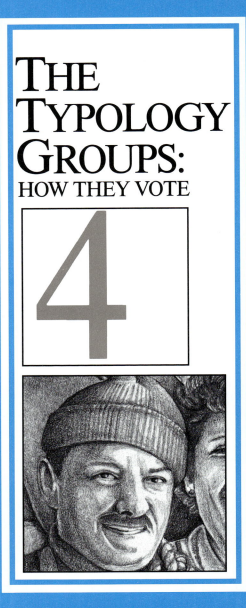

PARTY LOYALTY

The one thing party officials hate most is when their own faithful desert the fold. "Damn principles! Stick to your party." British Prime Minister Benjamin Disraeli could just as well have been speaking to American voters when he uttered those words. Some American voters are almost always loyal to their party, while others scarcely give it a second thought. Just look at the presidential votes of 1980 and 1984 and the congressional vote of 1986 listed by typology groups. (*See Figure 1.*)

Two points that emerge from Figure 1 are:

1) The party loyalty of the two bedrock GOP groups, Enterprisers and Moralists, is not only extremely high, but it also carries all the way through the 1986 congressional vote.

2) In contrast, the four Democratic core groups, Partisan Poor, Passive Poor, New Dealers and '60s Democrats, show significantly less party loyalty in the presidential contests than do their GOP counterparts. Democratic defection is especially critical among the Passive Poor and the New Dealers, with this latter group hurting the most since they are a very large segment of the population (11 percent) and an even larger bloc of likely voters (15 percent). The only good news for the Democrats is that many in these core groups who strayed to the GOP came back home by voting solidly Democratic in 1986.

FIGURE 1. PARTY LOYALTY*

1980 Vote	Reagan	Carter

	Reagan	Carter
TOTAL	51%	49%
ENTERPRISERS	93%	7%
MORALISTS	92%	8%
UPBEATS	78%	22%
DISAFFECTEDS	69%	31%
FOLLOWERS	40%	60%
SECULARS	29%	71%
'60s DEMOCRATS	18%	82%
NEW DEALERS	21%	79%
PASSIVE POOR	21%	79%
PARTISAN POOR	16%	84%

0 10 20 30 40 50 60 70 80 90 100

*Note: Based on major party vote.

FIGURE 1 (cont.) PARTY LOYALTY*

1984 Vote ▮ Reagan ▮ Mondale

TOTAL	58% / 42%
ENTERPRISERS	96% / 4%
MORALISTS	97% / 3%
UPBEATS	86% / 14%
DISAFFECTEDS	81% / 19%
FOLLOWERS	54% / 46%
SECULARS	34% / 66%
'60s DEMOCRATS	25% / 75%
NEW DEALERS	30% / 70%
PASSIVE POOR	31% / 69%
PARTISAN POOR	19% / 81%

0 10 20 30 40 50 60 70 80 90 100

*Note: Based on major party vote.

FIGURE 1 (cont.) PARTY LOYALTY*

1986 Congressional vote ▮ Republican ▮ Democrat

TOTAL	44% / 56%
ENTERPRISERS	89% / 11%
MORALISTS	95% / 5%
UPBEATS	64% / 36%
DISAFFECTEDS	57% / 43%
FOLLOWERS	35% / 65%
SECULARS	28% / 72%
'60s DEMOCRATS	15% / 85%
NEW DEALERS	8% / 92%
PASSIVE POOR	17% / 83%
PARTISAN POOR	95% / 5%

0 10 20 30 40 50 60 70 80 90 100

*Note: Based on major party vote.

"Democrats...who strayed to the GOP came back home by voting solidly Democratic in 1986."

FIGURE 2. PARTY IDENTIFICATION

	TOTAL	ENTERPRISERS	MORALISTS	UPBEATS	DISAFFECTEDS	BYSTANDERS	FOLLOWERS	SECULARS	'60s DEMOCRATS	NEW DEALERS	PASSIVE POOR	PARTISAN POOR
Republican and leaner	38%	99%	99%	66%	44%	29%	23%	16%	3%	0%	8%	1%
Republican	25%	77%	87%	33%	16%	16%	10%	8%	1%	0%	2%	0%
Lean Republican	13%	22%	12%	33%	28%	13%	13%	8%	2%	0%	6%	1%
Democrat and leaner	50%	*	0%	13%	26%	33%	55%	77%	90%	99%	87%	98%
Democrat	37%	*	0%	3%	6%	19%	39%	48%	62%	86%	70%	89%
Lean Democrat	13%	*	0%	10%	21%	14%	16%	29%	28%	13%	17%	9%
Independent	38%	23%	13%	63%	78%	65%	51%	44%	36%	14%	28%	11%
Refused to lean	12%	1%	1%	21%	30%	38%	22%	7%	7%	1%	5%	1%
	100%	100%	100%	100%	100%	100%	100%	100%	100%	100%	100%	100%

*Less than 0.5 percent.

PARTY IDENTIFICATION

The three groups that are upper-middle class and the most politically sophisticated—Enterprise Republicans, Seculars and '60s Democrats—do not display a rock solid affinity to the political parties with which they identify or lean. Even though Enterprisers vote strongly GOP, they are much less likely than Moralists to say they are strong Republicans. In a similar manner, much smaller proportions of '60s Democrats claim their affiliation with the party to be strong compared with other staunchly Democratic groups. While 90 percent of '60s Democrats are behavioral Democrats, 36 percent of them claim to be independent. While 77 percent of Seculars are or lean Democratic, 44 percent claim to be independent. (*See Figure 2.*)

REALIGNMENT

There is no evidence to suggest that the Reagan landslide of 1984 has led to a permanent partisan realignment. At the time of this survey (April-May 1987)—fully a year and a half from election day—the inroads Republicans made into traditional Democratic groups in 1980 and 1984 show no signs of automatically repeating.

When respondents were asked directly whether they were more likely to vote for a Republican or Democrat for president in 1988, the result is a predictable partisan alignment. (*See Figure 3.*)

FIGURE 3. LIKELY VOTE IN 1988 PRESIDENTIAL ELECTION

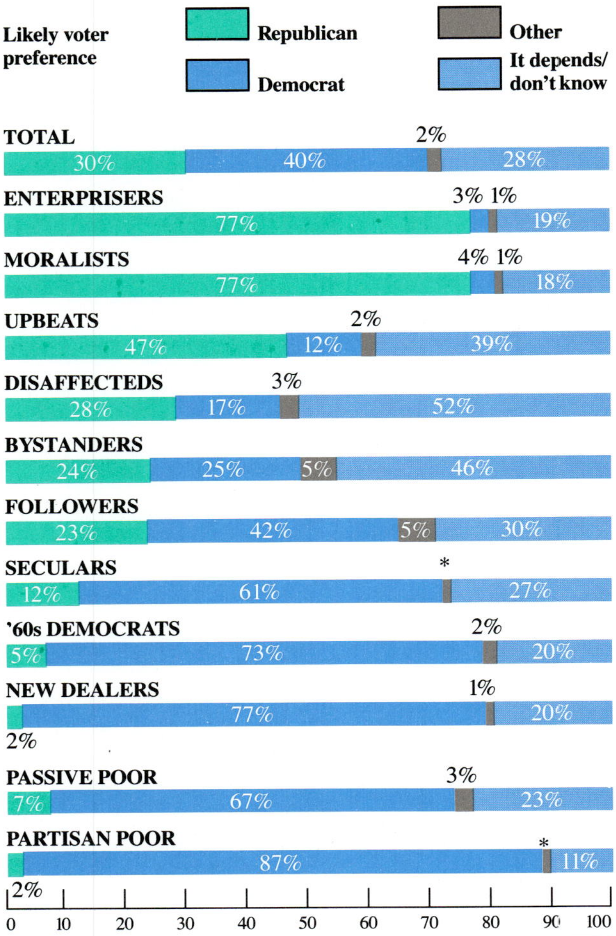

Likely voter preference

■ Republican ■ Other
■ Democrat ■ It depends/ don't know

Group	Republican	Democrat	Other	It depends/don't know
TOTAL	30%	40%	2%	28%
ENTERPRISERS	77%	3%	1%	19%
MORALISTS	77%	4%	1%	18%
UPBEATS	47%	12%	2%	39%
DISAFFECTEDS	28%	17%	3%	52%
BYSTANDERS	24%	25%	5%	46%
FOLLOWERS	23%	42%	5%	30%
SECULARS	12%	61%	*	27%
'60s DEMOCRATS	5%	73%	2%	20%
NEW DEALERS	2%	77%	1%	20%
PASSIVE POOR	7%	67%	3%	23%
PARTISAN POOR	2%	87%	*	11%

0 10 20 30 40 50 60 70 80 90 100

*Less than 0.5 percent.

TRIAL HEATS

Another measure of the strength of partisanship is candidate preferences in trial heat polls. Trial heats this far from election day are not intended to forecast results. Although name recognition plays a key role in these hypothetical matchups —especially so early in a campaign—as a measure of partisanship, trial heats help gauge the support of a "candidate like" the specific contender mentioned.

In our three presidential trial heats, the Democrat beats the Republican each time. (It is important to note that the field interviews for this survey were in process during the Gary Hart-Donna Rice episode. While the Hart withdrawal obviously affects our trial heats, it does not harm their basic goal—to measure leading Democrats versus leading Republicans and see how our typology groups divide. Without a Democratic front-runner, it would now be harder to gauge these choices.) Gary Hart leads George Bush by a margin of nine percentage points. Hart beats Robert Dole by 18 percentage points; Ted Kennedy beats Dole by 12 percentage points. More importantly, Republican and Republican-leaning groups support or lean toward Bush or Dole at levels consistent with their partisan affiliation, while Democrat and Democrat-leaning groups prefer Hart or Kennedy at levels reflecting their partisan affiliation.

Support for a candidate like Ted Kennedy is somewhat lower among '60s Democrats, Seculars and New Dealers than it is for a candidate like Gary Hart. However, a candidacy like Kennedy's would attract even higher proportions of the Partisan Poor, Followers and Passive Poor.

Higher numbers of Moralists choose Bush over Hart than prefer Dole over Hart, but preference for Dole goes up when the opponent is Kennedy. A plurality of Upbeats would vote for Bush or Dole, though fewer would vote for Kennedy than Hart. A Kennedy candidacy would also mobilize the Disaffecteds against the Democrats.

At the time of the poll, neither Republican candidate had yet to spark enthusiasm among Upbeats or the other independent groups that Republicans vitally need for victory. Nor had Dole achieved a high level of support among the Moralists. Unlike Ronald Reagan, neither Bush nor Dole yet seems able to make inroads with the New Dealers, who are another GOP electoral target.

The Kennedy trial heat is important because it shows that a candidate like the Massachusetts Senator will drive the Seculars *away* from the Democratic Party. But even Moral Republicans show their tendency toward populism, as one in five choose Kennedy over Dole. (*See Figure 4.*)

FIGURE 4. 1988 PRESIDENTIAL TRIAL HEATS*

	TOTAL	ENTERPRISERS	MORALISTS	UPBEATS	DISAFFECTEDS	BYSTANDERS	FOLLOWERS	SECULARS	'60s DEMOCRATS	NEW DEALERS	PASSIVE POOR	PARTISAN POOR
Trial Heats												
Bush	40%	82%	78%	50%	41%	41%	30%	23%	14%	19%	25%	14%
Hart	49%	14%	14%	40%	45%	30%	47%	69%	80%	75%	65%	80%
Other/ undecided	11%	4%	8%	10%	14%	29%	23%	8%	6%	6%	10%	6%
Dole	34%	79%	68%	43%	33%	20%	19%	30%	21%	16%	17%	11%
Hart	52%	15%	19%	43%	50%	44%	51%	64%	71%	75%	73%	79%
Other/ undecided	14%	6%	13%	14%	17%	36%	30%	6%	8%	9%	10%	10%
Dole	39%	89%	73%	48%	49%	20%	21%	40%	27%	23%	16%	9%
Kennedy	51%	8%	20%	42%	38%	55%	61%	50%	67%	71%	78%	86%
Other/ undecided	10%	3%	7%	10%	13%	25%	18%	10%	6%	6%	6%	5%

*Note: Includes leaners.

THE TYPOLOGY GROUPS:
WHAT THEY THINK

5

REPUBLICAN IMAGE

Three terms come to mind most often when people are asked what it means to them when someone says they are a Republican: conservative (21 percent), money/power (18 percent) and business oriented (13 percent). Core Democratic groups mention money/power most often. Compared to other groups, significantly higher proportions of Seculars are the only group to name business oriented as the meaning of being a Republican. *(See Figure 5.)*

DEMOCRATIC IMAGE

The public most often defines being a Democrat as being for working people/people oriented (21 percent) or a liberal (18 percent). Republican groups—Enterprisers (35 percent) and Moralists (25 percent)—mention liberal in significantly higher proportions, as do Seculars (32 percent) and '60s Democrats (29 percent). *(See Figure 5, continued on next page.)*

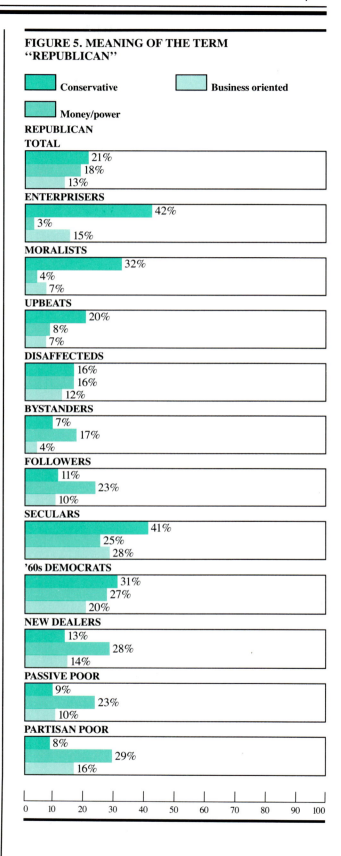

FIGURE 5. MEANING OF THE TERM "REPUBLICAN"

■ Conservative   ■ Business oriented   ■ Money/power

REPUBLICAN

TOTAL
- Conservative: 21%
- Business oriented: 18%
- Money/power: 13%

ENTERPRISERS
- Conservative: 42%
- Business oriented: 3%
- Money/power: 15%

MORALISTS
- Conservative: 32%
- Business oriented: 4%
- Money/power: 7%

UPBEATS
- Conservative: 20%
- Business oriented: 8%
- Money/power: 7%

DISAFFECTEDS
- Conservative: 16%
- Business oriented: 16%
- Money/power: 12%

BYSTANDERS
- Conservative: 7%
- Business oriented: 17%
- Money/power: 4%

FOLLOWERS
- Conservative: 11%
- Business oriented: 23%
- Money/power: 10%

SECULARS
- Conservative: 41%
- Business oriented: 25%
- Money/power: 28%

'60s DEMOCRATS
- Conservative: 31%
- Business oriented: 27%
- Money/power: 20%

NEW DEALERS
- Conservative: 13%
- Business oriented: 28%
- Money/power: 14%

PASSIVE POOR
- Conservative: 9%
- Business oriented: 23%
- Money/power: 10%

PARTISAN POOR
- Conservative: 8%
- Business oriented: 29%
- Money/power: 16%

0 10 20 30 40 50 60 70 80 90 100

FIGURE 5 (cont.) MEANING OF THE TERM "DEMOCRAT"

■ For working people/people oriented   ■ Person who votes Democratic/believes in the party

■ Liberal

DEMOCRAT

TOTAL
- 21%
- 18%
- 9%

ENTERPRISERS
- 9%
- 35%
- 6%

MORALISTS
- 7%
- 25%
- 5%

UPBEATS
- 13%
- 17%
- 8%

DISAFFECTEDS
- 13%
- 12%
- 11%

BYSTANDERS
- 13%
- 8%
- 9%

FOLLOWERS
- 22%
- 9%
- 19%

SECULARS
- 30%
- 32%
- 6%

'60s DEMOCRATS
- 31%
- 29%
- 8%

NEW DEALERS
- 35%
- 14%
- 11%

PASSIVE POOR
- 26%
- 10%
- 8%

PARTISAN POOR
- 34%
- 9%
- 14%

0 10 20 30 40 50 60 70 80 90 100

LEADING NATIONAL PROBLEM

Economic concerns are cited as the most important problem facing the country today. However, except for times of major international tension, economic problems nearly always dominate this traditional Gallup question. For this survey, unemployment/recession/depression is volunteered by 13 percent. Two groups that single out unemployment—the Partisan Poor and Passive Poor—are obviously those who are most directly concerned with this problem. Enterprisers and Seculars are the two groups that mention the federal budget deficit/failure to balance the budget in proportions higher than average. Followers say drug abuse is the nation's most important problem. (*See Figure 6.*)

"*Economic concerns are cited as the most important problem facing the country today.*"

FIGURE 6. THE NATION'S MOST IMPORTANT PROBLEM

	TOTAL	ENTERPRISERS	MORALISTS	UPBEATS	DISAFFECTEDS	BYSTANDERS	FOLLOWERS	SECULARS	'60s DEMOCRATS	NEW DEALERS	PASSIVE POOR	PARTISAN POOR
Unemployment/ recession/ depression	13%	6%	11%	8%	16%	14%	9%	8%	8%	20%	20%	25%
Federal budget deficit/failure to balance the budget	12%	30%	14%	11%	12%	3%	6%	17%	12%	12%	7%	6%
Threat/fear of (nuclear) war	7%	4%	8%	9%	6%	10%	9%	9%	8%	7%	5%	6%
Economy	7%	9%	6%	10%	9%	3%	2%	8%	9%	8%	6%	10%
Poverty/hunger	6%	2%	3%	8%	3%	10%	6%	5%	6%	7%	6%	8%
Drug abuse	6%	3%	6%	5%	3%	8%	13%	2%	2%	5%	7%	6%
Arms race	4%	2%	3%	5%	3%	4%	2%	8%	6%	4%	3%	3%
Foreign affairs/ policy/inter- national problems	3%	3%	3%	5%	2%	4%	4%	5%	3%	3%	4%	2%
Crime	3%	2%	2%	2%	2%	5%	10%	2%	2%	3%	4%	3%
Trade deficit/ trade problems	3%	6%	3%	5%	2%	2%	1%	3%	5%	2%	2%	3%

PARTY COMPETENCY

A follow-up question asks which party is better able to handle the leading problem cited by each person. The Gallup Poll trend for this question shows a clear *decline* in confidence in the Republican Party's ability to handle the leading problem. Since 1985, feelings on this question have reversed. Today, 38 percent say the Democratic Party is best able to handle the leading problem, an increase of 9 percentage points in only two years. The Republican Party does *not* achieve very much support beyond its most solid constituency—Enterprisers (73 percent) and Moralists (66 percent). Except for a moderate level of support from Upbeats (42 percent), very low votes of confidence are given to the GOP's problem-solving ability. On the other hand, the Democratic Party not only receives solid support from its bedrock groups—Partisan Poor (73 percent), Passive Poor (63 percent), New Dealers (67 percent) and '60s Democrats (62 percent), but the party also gets a substantial vote of confidence from Seculars (52 percent). (*See Figure 7.*)

FIGURE 7. POLITICAL PARTY BETTER ABLE TO HANDLE THE NATION'S MOST IMPORTANT PROBLEM

■ Republican	■ No difference
■ Democrat	■ Don't know

CURRENT
28% | 38% | 24% | 10%

JULY 1986*
33% | 36% | 21% | 10%

JANUARY 1985*
39% | 29% | 24% | 8%

ENTERPRISERS
73% | 6% | 16% | 5%

MORALISTS
66% | 5% | 21% | 8%

UPBEATS
42% | 19% | 28% | 11%

DISAFFECTEDS
27% | 25% | 36% | 12%

BYSTANDERS
19% | 26% | 8% | 17%

FOLLOWERS
15% | 40% | 29% | 16%

SECULARS
15% | 52% | 24% | 9%

'60s DEMOCRATS
8% | 62% | 22% | 8%

NEW DEALERS
5% | 67% | 18% | 10%

PASSIVE POOR
12% | 63% | 16% | 9%

PARTISAN POOR
5% | 73% | 15% | 7%

0 10 20 30 40 50 60 70 80 90 100

*Gallup trend.

PARTY TRAITS

Respondents were asked whether each of the following phrases best describes the Democratic Party or the Republican Party.

Is well organized? One-third of the general population feels this term describes the Republican Party. Enterprisers (56 percent), Moralists (58 percent) and Upbeats (44 percent) are more likely than average to feel the Republican Party is well organized. Most impressive is the high proportion of '60s Democrats (46 percent) who also say the Republicans are well organized.

Selects good candidates for office? While people attribute this quality to both parties, most revealing is the relatively low numbers of '60s Democrats and Seculars who say this describes their party. This relatively low opinion of its own candidates shows serious signs of disaffection among the most sophisticated elements of the Democratic Party.

Is concerned with the needs and interests of the disadvantaged? Most Americans (61 percent) say this phrase describes the Democratic Party. However, Moralists attribute this quality to the Republican Party in proportions three times the national average (33 percent vs. 11 percent).

Is forward looking, not old-fashioned? A small plurality of Americans feel this best describes the Democratic Party (38 percent). The typology groups divide along partisan lines.

Has a common-sense approach to problems? Thirty-five percent say the Democrats, 28 percent say Republicans. Most serious for the Democrats, Seculars do *not* join with the other Democratic groups in saying this quality best describes the Democratic Party. Once again, the Seculars, a group the Democrats vitally need, show disaffection with the party.

Is able to manage the federal government well? Overall responses divide equally, at one-quarter for each party. Disaffecteds, Seculars and to a lesser degree '60s Democrats and Enterprisers feel neither party is able to manage the federal government well.

Can bring about the kinds of changes the country needs? Thirty-six percent feel this best describes the Democratic Party, 26 percent say the Republican Party. The Democrats receive very high levels of confidence from the Partisan Poor (76 percent).

Is concerned with the needs and interests of business and other powerful groups? Fifty-eight percent feel this best describes the Republican Party. Disproportionately higher numbers of '60s Democrats (83 percent) and Seculars (76 percent) see this as a quality of the GOP. Of interest are the significantly higher-than-average proportions of Passive Poor (32 percent) and Partisan Poor (24 percent) who feel this best describes the *Democratic* Party. (*See Figure 8.*)

FIGURE 8. PHRASES THAT BEST DESCRIBE THE REPUBLICAN OR DEMOCRATIC PARTY

	TOTAL	ENTERPRISERS	MORALISTS	UPBEATS	DISAFFECTEDS	BYSTANDERS	FOLLOWERS	SECULARS	'60s DEMOCRATS	NEW DEALERS	PASSIVE POOR	PARTISAN POOR
Well organized												
Republican	34%	56%	58%	44%	28%	20%	16%	38%	46%	20%	21%	21%
Democratic	19%	4%	4%	9%	14%	18%	33%	9%	12%	32%	61%	39%
Selects good candidates for office												
Republican	27%	55%	63%	39%	30%	19%	18%	15%	15%	8%	16%	10%
Democratic	26%	3%	3%	10%	12%	22%	32%	32%	33%	46%	53%	54%
Concerned with needs/interests of disadvantaged												
Republican	11%	12%	33%	20%	13%	12%	13%	2%	3%	2%	5%	3%
Democratic	61%	57%	30%	46%	49%	39%	50%	80%	89%	82%	75%	86%
Forward looking, not old-fashioned												
Republican	27%	52%	61%	40%	25%	21%	16%	11%	10%	14%	17%	13%
Democratic	38%	13%	13%	23%	27%	24%	37%	57%	60%	58%	58%	64%
Common-sense approach to problems												
Republican	28%	70%	71%	41%	27%	21%	15%	18%	12%	4%	11%	4%
Democratic	35%	4%	4%	17%	19%	23%	38%	39%	55%	67%	62%	73%
Able to manage federal government well												
Republican	25%	55%	60%	41%	18%	19%	15%	11%	12%	5%	12%	7%
Democratic	25%	1%	3%	7%	10%	19%	33%	24%	31%	51%	51%	55%
Can bring about changes country needs												
Republican	26%	67%	68%	41%	22%	20%	16%	10%	7%	4%	8%	3%
Democratic	36%	3%	3%	13%	18%	22%	42%	50%	60%	70%	64%	76%
Concerned with needs/interests of powerful groups												
Republican	58%	67%	65%	58%	51%	36%	38%	76%	83%	60%	42%	57%
Democratic	15%	6%	9%	11%	12%	14%	20%	9%	7%	22%	32%	24%

KEY POLITICAL EVENTS

Respondents were asked to choose among 13 events (from the Depression through the Reagan presidency) that most shaped their political views. Their answers show the profound effect the Vietnam War had on the American political psyche. Twenty percent chose Vietnam as the political event that most shaped their views, nearly twice as many mentions as any other event. Eight of the 11 typology groups rank Vietnam first. The exceptions are the Partisan Poor, who cited the JFK presidency, and the Passive Poor and New Dealers, who list the Depression as the key event.

References to John F. Kennedy—whether to his presidency or assassination—together receive a very high percentage of mentions from the Partisan Poor, Passive Poor, New Dealers and '60s Democrats. "Camelot" is more than just a political catchphrase—it lives on in the minds of many in these groups. (*See Figure 9.*)

FIGURE 9. MAJOR EVENTS THAT SHAPED POLITICAL VIEWS

Event	TOTAL	ENTERPRISERS	MORALISTS	UPBEATS	DISAFFECTEDS	BYSTANDERS	FOLLOWERS	SECULARS	'60s DEMOCRATS	NEW DEALERS	PASSIVE POOR	PARTISAN POOR
The Vietnam War	20%	21%	16%	24%	25%	21%	17%	24%	26%	12%	15%	15%
The Great Depression	12%	12%	15%	9%	10%	8%	7%	7%	9%	19%	19%	12%
The Ronald Reagan presidency	10%	15%	14%	17%	6%	11%	4%	9%	8%	6%	7%	6%
The John F. Kennedy presidency	9%	4%	6%	8%	10%	7%	10%	8%	9%	13%	12%	16%
Assassinations of the 1960s—John and Robert Kennedy and Martin Luther King, Jr.	8%	2%	7%	8%	7%	9%	9%	5%	11%	10%	13%	12%
World War II	7%	8%	11%	7%	8%	5%	7%	4%	7%	7%	7%	3%
The Civil Rights movement	7%	5%	5%	6%	3%	6%	9%	10%	13%	6%	10%	12%
The Watergate crisis	6%	4%	6%	6%	7%	7%	4%	11%	6%	6%	3%	5%
FDR and the New Deal	5%	9%	3%	2%	6%	1%	5%	7%	4%	7%	4%	5%
The Jimmy Carter presidency	3%	7%	5%	2%	4%	2%	3%	3%	1%	2%	2%	2%
The Holocaust	2%	1%	2%	5%	3%	2%	3%	5%	2%	1%	3%	2%
The Korean War	2%	3%	2%	1%	2%	1%	3%	1%	1%	3%	1%	1%
The McCarthy era	1%	1%	1%	*	1%	*	1%	1%	1%	1%	0%	1%
Don't know	8%	8%	7%	5%	8%	20%	18%	5%	2%	7%	4%	8%
	100%	100%	100%	100%	100%	100%	100%	100%	100%	100%	100%	100%

*Less than 0.5 percent.

RATING PEOPLE AND INSTITUTIONS

People were asked to rate a number of personalities and institutions. Overall, the living Americans rated *very* favorable include Lee Iacocca (24 percent), Dan Rather (24 percent), Billy Graham (22 percent), Oprah Winfrey (22 percent), Ted Kennedy (21 percent) and Ronald Reagan (21 percent). Institutions rated *very* favorable include: daily newspapers (22 percent), network television news (21 percent), the military (17 percent), the Supreme Court (13 percent) and Congress (10 percent). (*See Figures 10 and 11.*)

FIGURE 10. FAVORABILITY RATINGS OF PERSONALITIES—"VERY FAVORABLE RATINGS"

	TOTAL	ENTERPRISERS	MORALISTS	UPBEATS	DISAFFECTEDS	BYSTANDERS	FOLLOWERS	SECULARS	'60s DEMOCRATS	NEW DEALERS	PASSIVE POOR	PARTISAN POOR
Lee Iacocca	24%	39%	28%	29%	25%	16%	10%	26%	30%	19%	23%	18%
Dan Rather	24%	15%	23%	27%	23%	21%	17%	19%	28%	33%	31%	27%
Billy Graham	22%	29%	41%	21%	26%	14%	13%	4%	17%	29%	19%	22%
Oprah Winfrey	22%	13%	18%	19%	20%	23%	21%	16%	27%	18%	34%	38%
Ted Kennedy	21%	2%	10%	15%	15%	21%	23%	14%	23%	32%	40%	48%
Ronald Reagan	21%	42%	53%	32%	18%	17%	13%	7%	6%	9%	10%	6%
Gary Hart	15%	5%	7%	9%	11%	26%	9%	15%	15%	22%	23%	27%
Jimmy Carter	14%	3%	7%	9%	9%	10%	15%	13%	24%	22%	25%	22%
Jesse Jackson	13%	4%	6%	6%	4%	12%	17%	7%	22%	13%	27%	31%
George Bush	11%	20%	29%	13%	10%	11%	7%	2%	4%	6%	8%	6%
Robert Dole	9%	17%	17%	9%	7%	6%	8%	6%	7%	10%	7%	5%
Richard Nixon	7%	10%	12%	9%	7%	8%	4%	3%	3%	4%	7%	4%
Geraldine Ferraro	6%	1%	5%	3%	4%	4%	7%	8%	15%	8%	8%	10%

FIGURE 11. FAVORABILITY RATINGS

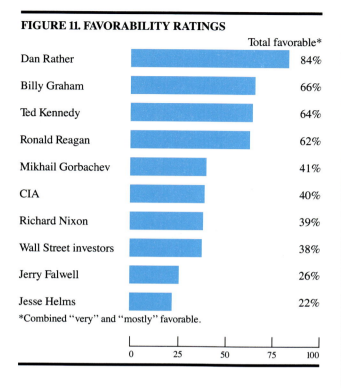

Total favorable*

Dan Rather	84%
Billy Graham	66%
Ted Kennedy	64%
Ronald Reagan	62%
Mikhail Gorbachev	41%
CIA	40%
Richard Nixon	39%
Wall Street investors	38%
Jerry Falwell	26%
Jesse Helms	22%

*Combined "very" and "mostly" favorable.

0   25   50   75   100

"Glasnost must be working since Gorbachev receives favorable ratings, larger than Richard Nixon, Jerry Falwell or Jesse Helms."

FIGURE 12. FAVORABILITY RATINGS OF INSTITUTIONS—"VERY FAVORABLE RATINGS"

	TOTAL	ENTERPRISERS	MORALISTS	UPBEATS	DISAFFECTEDS	BYSTANDERS	FOLLOWERS	SECULARS	'60s DEMOCRATS	NEW DEALERS	PASSIVE POOR	PARTISAN POOR
Daily newspaper you are most familiar with	22%	16%	22%	18%	19%	26%	16%	21%	23%	29%	28%	22%
Network TV news	21%	13%	19%	22%	18%	26%	9%	14%	26%	33%	31%	23%
Military	17%	20%	23%	20%	14%	17%	8%	7%	18%	20%	21%	16%
The nuclear freeze movement	16%	12%	12%	17%	18%	12%	11%	21%	27%	14%	13%	18%
The Supreme Court	13%	12%	16%	13%	8%	17%	13%	9%	13%	17%	10%	11%
The Congress	10%	4%	14%	12%	9%	12%	6%	7%	15%	15%	7%	5%
Lawyers	7%	3%	8%	10%	2%	11%	7%	5%	5%	15%	7%	8%
Wall Street investors	5%	5%	3%	4%	4%	10%	4%	2%	4%	6%	7%	6%
CIA	4%	2%	8%	5%	2%	5%	*	2%	5%	6%	5%	6%

*Less than 0.5 percent.

Glasnost must be working since Mikhail Gorbachev receives a *combined* favorable rating ("very" and "mostly") of 41 percent, larger than the scores of Richard Nixon, Jerry Falwell or Jesse Helms. Gorbachev also receives a higher combined favorable rating than the CIA and Wall Street investors. (*See Figure 12.*)

Enterprisers give *very* favorable ratings in the highest proportions to Reagan (42 percent). George Bush (20 percent) receives a relatively low level of very favorable responses from this Republican group, and Robert Dole (17 percent) does not fair well, either. Moralists rate Bush (29 percent) very favorable in much larger proportions than Enterprisers, but give similarly low levels of very favorable ratings to Dole (17 percent). Moralists rate Reagan 11 percentage points higher than do the Enterprisers—again showing lower levels of *strong* support for the Republican Party and its leaders by the Enterprisers.

Four Democratic groups—'60s Democrats (24 percent), New Dealers (24 percent), Passive Poor (25 percent) and the Partisan Poor (22 percent)—rate Jimmy Carter very favorable, but the Seculars (13 percent) are less inclined to do so. Jesse Jackson receives strong favorability ratings from the Partisan Poor (31 percent), Passive Poor (27 percent) and '60s Democrats (24 percent), but not from the less racially tolerant New Dealers (13 percent) or the Seculars (7 percent). Ted Kennedy receives very favorable ratings from the Partisan Poor (48 percent) and Passive Poor (40 percent), but *not* from the Seculars (14 percent).

THE TYPOLOGY GROUPS:
ISSUES & SHIFTING COALITIONS

The typology goes beyond just describing political party preferences. It reveals a surprising and shifting group of coalitions across a broad array of social and political dimensions. The coalitions change dramatically on fundamental beliefs about tolerance, social justice, foreign policy and more. Members of typology groups considered quite divergent join together into blocs sharing common views on such issues as abortion, environment, school prayer, mandatory drug tests, aid to the Contras, the death penalty, AIDS, military spending and arms control.

When voters align into coalitions on specific issues without regard to party, the results can be quite dramatic.

INTOLERANCE COALITIONS

Intolerance represents the belief in *less* personal freedom for those who do not share the intolerant individual's values. Intolerant people go further than simply showing disapproval of the ideas or lifestyles with which they disagree. They have a moral certainty and actually want to impose their view of the world on others. The intolerant coalition probably made up a large part of George Wallace's support in 1968 and 1972. And today, this coalition is one of the reasons for Ronald Reagan's electoral success. Two groups traditionally relied on by the Democrats—New Dealers and Passive Poor—share the low tolerance of Moral Republicans. And Reagan's rhetorical stress on traditional, conservative values caused sharp Democratic defections in both groups. Although Enterprise Republicans are more likely to have tolerant attitudes, their level does not match the strongly tolerant views of '60s Democrats and Seculars.

Banning Books

Even though freedom of expression and freedom of the press are fundamental principles of American democracy, one out of two Americans feels that books containing dangerous ideas should be banned from public school libraries (51 percent). More than three out of four Passive Poor (82 percent), Moralists (77 percent) and New Dealers (74 percent) would censor "dangerous ideas." At the other extreme, '60s Democrats (10 percent) and Seculars (13 percent) show almost universal tolerance toward different ideas. Enterprisers (28 percent) also reject intolerance in very large numbers, as do the Upbeats (41 percent). (*See Figure 13.*)

FIGURE 13. INTOLERANCE COALITIONS*

	TOTAL	ENTERPRISERS	MORALISTS	UPBEATS	DISAFFECTEDS	BYSTANDERS	FOLLOWERS	SECULARS	'60s DEMOCRATS	NEW DEALERS	PASSIVE POOR	PARTISAN POOR
Banning books Agree that books containing dangerous ideas should be banned from public school libraries	51%	28%	77%	41%	52%	58%	57%	13%	10%	74%	82%	58%
School prayer Favor constitutional amendment to permit prayer in public schools	71%	69%	88%	77%	78%	69%	61%	30%	52%	83%	83%	81%
Homosexuality School boards have right to fire teachers who are known homosexuals	52%	50%	78%	35%	65%	54%	53%	18%	14%	69%	67%	51%
AIDS AIDS might be God's punishment for immoral sexual behavior	44%	36%	61%	32%	47%	50%	54%	8%	15%	56%	58%	55%
Drug testing Favor mandatory drug test for government employees	65%	58%	80%	65%	70%	68%	64%	39%	39%	78%	77%	69%
Attitudes toward women and abortion Agree women should return to traditional role in society	30%	16%	47%	14%	34%	32%	41%	8%	5%	47%	46%	31%
Favor changing laws to make it more difficult for a woman to get an abortion	41%	40%	60%	40%	44%	37%	43%	13%	26%	54%	47%	38%
Strongly self-identify as supporter of the anti-abortion movement	32%	29%	45%	22%	35%	31%	28%	10%	24%	40%	40%	38%

*HOW TO READ THE TABLE: Example: 28 percent of Enterprisers agree that books containing dangerous ideas should be banned from public school libraries.

FIGURE 13. INTOLERANCE COALITIONS* (cont'd.)

	TOTAL	ENTERPRISERS	MORALISTS	UPBEATS	DISAFFECTEDS	BYSTANDERS	FOLLOWERS	SECULARS	'60s DEMOCRATS	NEW DEALERS	PASSIVE POOR	PARTISAN POOR
Race												
Agree that it's all right for blacks and whites to date each other	48%	55%	25%	46%	30%	48%	50%	73%	78%	28%	56%	52%
Favor increased spending on programs that assist minorities	36%	12%	21%	27%	17%	40%	42%	40%	50%	39%	57%	60%
Strongly self-identify as supporter of civil rights movement	47%	32%	33%	46%	33%	41%	38%	60%	77%	40%	62%	66%

School Prayer

On a constitutional amendment to permit prayer in public schools, Moralists (88 percent) are joined by the Passive Poor (83 percent), New Dealers (83 percent) and the Partisan Poor (81 percent) in favoring such an amendment. Seculars (30 percent) are most likely to oppose the amendment.

Homosexuality

Moralists (78 percent), New Dealers (69 percent) and Passive Poor (67 percent) feel school boards should fire known homosexual teachers. Sixties Democrats (14 percent), Seculars (18 percent) and, to a lesser extent, Upbeats (35 percent) do not hold that view in large numbers. However, few Americans are willing to call themselves supporters of the gay rights movement—only 8 percent of the general population. But among the most tolerant groups—'60s Democrats (21 percent) and Seculars (22 percent)—one in five strongly identifies with that movement.

AIDS

Considering AIDS to be God's punishment for immoral sexual behavior adds the religious factor to intolerance for homosexuality. The Partisan Poor (55 percent) join the other intolerant groups—Moralists, Passive Poor and New Dealers—in agreeing to the connection between AIDS and God's wrath. However, '60s Democrats (15 percent) do not accept the religious connection between AIDS and sexual behavior.

Drug Testing

Another contemporary issue on imposing limits on personal freedom involves the right of privacy versus the right of employers to screen drug users from the work place. On mandatory drug tests for government employees, the intolerance coalition holds firm—Moralists (80 percent), New Dealers (78 percent) and Passive Poor (77 percent) agree with this proposal. Fewer than two in five '60s Democrats (39 percent) and Seculars (39 percent) agree with mandatory tests.

Role of Women

The Intolerance/Tolerance coalitions are most clearly defined by attitudes about the role of women in society and abortion. Moralists, New Dealers and Passive Poor combine as the groups more likely to agree that women should return to their traditional role in society; more likely to agree to changing the laws to make it *more difficult* for a woman to get an abortion; and more likely to strongly self-identify as a supporter of the anti-abortion movement. Seculars, '60s Democrats and Upbeats are more likely to hold the opposite viewpoint in all three cases.

Race

The issue of racial intolerance creates a somewhat different combination of groupings. About one-half of the general population feels that it's "all right" for blacks and whites to date each other. Moralists (25 percent), New Dealers (28 percent) and Disaffecteds (30 percent) are the groups *least* likely to agree with interracial dating. Approximately three-fourths of the '60s Democrats (78 percent) and Seculars (73 percent) are tolerant on blacks and whites dating.

Opinions about racial tolerance are mixed among the three groups with the largest numbers of blacks—Partisan Poor (52 percent), Passive Poor (56 percent) and Followers (50 percent). This conflict is because of the whites who compose the largest percentage of these groups; this is especially true among the Passive Poor, where mild expressions of racial prejudice spill over to attitudes about social programs that deal with equal opportunity.

The racial prejudice of the New Dealers collides with their strong, positive attitudes about government intervention to achieve social justice. As a result, New Dealers back social justice measures only when they are not specifically targeted to blacks and other minorities.

SOCIAL JUSTICE COALITIONS

Three in five (62 percent) Americans surveyed firmly believe that achieving social justice should be one of the government's primary goals. The Social Justice coalition is strong. Only two typology groups disagree with the view that the government should guarantee every citizen enough to eat and a place to sleep: Enterprisers (24 percent) and Disaffecteds (49 percent). Passive Poor (92 percent) and the Partisan Poor (81 percent) most consistently agree that it is the government's role to provide a safety net. (*See Figure 14.*)

FIGURE 14. SOCIAL JUSTICE COALITIONS

	TOTAL	ENTERPRISERS	MORALISTS	UPBEATS	DISAFFECTEDS	BYSTANDERS	FOLLOWERS	SECULARS	'60s DEMOCRATS	NEW DEALERS	PASSIVE POOR	PARTISAN POOR
Agree that the government should guarantee every citizen enough to eat and a place to sleep	62%	24%	55%	63%	49%	70%	64%	63%	67%	67%	92%	81%
Favor increased spending on...												
Programs for the elderly	75%	44%	71%	76%	76%	81%	72%	74%	79%	84%	84%	87%
Programs for the homeless	68%	38%	62%	64%	61%	74%	69%	69%	77%	73%	82%	83%
Social Security	64%	29%	57%	65%	62%	70%	66%	53%	62%	76%	81%	85%
Programs for the unemployed	41%	11%	30%	30%	33%	51%	49%	38%	40%	49%	62%	68%
Improving nation's health care	71%	42%	68%	71%	69%	75%	67%	75%	76%	80%	85%	84%
Research on AIDS	68%	60%	64%	73%	66%	61%	69%	69%	76%	71%	74%	76%
Programs to reduce drug addiction	66%	49%	68%	68%	62%	68%	62%	57%	68%	77%	75%	74%
Aid to farmers	58%	29%	60%	59%	56%	66%	52%	44%	62%	69%	72%	70%

Social Programs

The strength of the Social Justice coalition varies across specific social programs, especially on the issues of race and aid to farmers.

Positions on relative levels of spending for the elderly, the homeless, Social Security and the unemployed confirm the general pattern of commitment to social justice. The Partisan Poor, Passive Poor, New Dealers and Bystanders join as the groups most likely to support these programs. Not surprisingly, these groups are composed of the poorest part of our population.

Enterprisers are solidly opposed to government spending to achieve social justice. This group stands quite apart from all others in their united position against every aspect of government sponsorship of social programs.

The Social Justice coalitions described above generally hold steady on the issue of improving the nation's health. Moreover, every constituency displays high levels of support for increasing the budget for AIDS research. Even three in five Enterprisers (60 percent) favor this measure.

Race

The race issue seriously divides the pro-social justice groups. The social justice beliefs of the New Deal Democrats decline sharply on questions of civil rights and programs focused on minorities. While three in five Passive Poor (57 percent) and Partisan Poor (60 percent) favor increasing federal spending on programs that assist blacks and other minorities, only two in five New Dealers (39 percent) approve of increasing funds.

More evidence on the split over civil rights is shown by the self-designated identification of being a supporter of the civil rights movement. The proportion of New Dealers (40 percent) who strongly identify with the civil rights movement is closer to the Moralists (33 percent) than to the Social Justice coalition.

FOREIGN POLICY COALITIONS

These coalitions center around three themes: attitudes about communism and ethnocentrism, opinions about military aggression and methods of achieving peace.

Across these three themes, Moralists lead the coalition that advocates a strong defense and a ready willingness to use force if necessary, a fear of communist aggression, a suspicion of the Russians, an unwillingness to compromise and an insistence on participating in arms reductions talks only from a position of power, if not superiority. New Dealers and Disaffecteds support this point of view and Enterprisers often lean in this direction.

Sixties Democrats and Seculars spearhead the types that join to encourage a tolerance of communism, a peace-oriented philosophy that favors cuts in defense spending, a reluctance to use military force and a willingness to compromise with the Russians to negotiate arms reductions, if not a nuclear freeze.

Moralists and New Dealers are staunch anti-communists. Disaffecteds, and to some extent the Passive Poor, combine with Moralists and New Dealers to form the anti-communist alliance. Substantial proportions of these groups agree with the statement that "the communists are responsible for a lot of the unrest in the U.S. today." In addition, significantly larger proportions of Moralists, New Dealers and Disaffecteds give the Soviet Union an unfavorable rating than do the other groups. More than four out of five Moralists (86 percent), New Dealers (84 percent) and Disaffecteds (83 percent) personally identify themselves as an anti-communist. Enterprisers (87 percent) are the most likely group to self-identify as anti-communist, while Passive Poor are the least inclined to do so. Sixties Democrats and Seculars represent the opposite end of the anti-communist spectrum, as significantly smaller percentages of them attribute American unrest to the communists. (*See Figure 15.*)

FIGURE 15. FOREIGN POLICY COALITIONS

	TOTAL	ENTERPRISERS	MORALISTS	UPBEATS	DISAFFECTEDS	BYSTANDERS	FOLLOWERS	SECULARS	'60s DEMOCRATS	NEW DEALERS	PASSIVE POOR	PARTISAN POOR
Attitudes toward communists												
Communist countries are all alike	37%	21%	59%	29%	43%	39%	35%	10%	9%	48%	61%	46%
Agree that communist countries are responsible for a lot of unrest in U.S. today	56%	47%	88%	46%	64%	54%	38%	20%	18%	79%	75%	67%
Unfavorable opinion of Soviet Union	71%	72%	84%	66%	81%	71%	76%	55%	53%	78%	68%	74%
Strongly self-identify as anti-communist	70%	87%	86%	71%	83%	57%	46%	46%	58%	84%	57%	71%
Nicaragua												
Favor increased aid to the Contras	9%	17%	18%	8%	8%	8%	8%	5%	2%	7%	10%	8%
U.S. should assist Contras	26%	52%	45%	34%	25%	13%	20%	15%	14%	21%	20%	15%

Nicaragua

When these attitudes about communism are tested in the context of our current Nicaragua policy, the solidarity of the anti-communist coalition is reduced by partisan allegiances. While only nine percent of the total sample would increase aid to the Contras, twice as many of the solidly Republican typology groups would increase Contra aid. New Dealers do *not* share the view of their anti-communist allies in significantly high proportions. Sixties Democrats and Seculars, adopting a position consistent with both their partisan alignment and their position on communism, lead the call for decreasing funds to the Contras. Even when the question of Contra aid is cast in the context of "guerilla forces now opposing the Marxist government in Nicaragua," the partisan alignment, rather than the anti-communist lineup, prevails.

One-half of the respondents (51 percent) think poverty and lack of human rights cause the unrest in Central America. Fewer than one in five Americans (19 percent) feel unrest in that region stems from Cuban, Nicaraguan and Soviet subversion.

Clearly, policy toward Central America follows the partisan alignment. Anti-communist New Dealers (53 percent) say poverty and

FIGURE 16. CENTRAL AMERICA

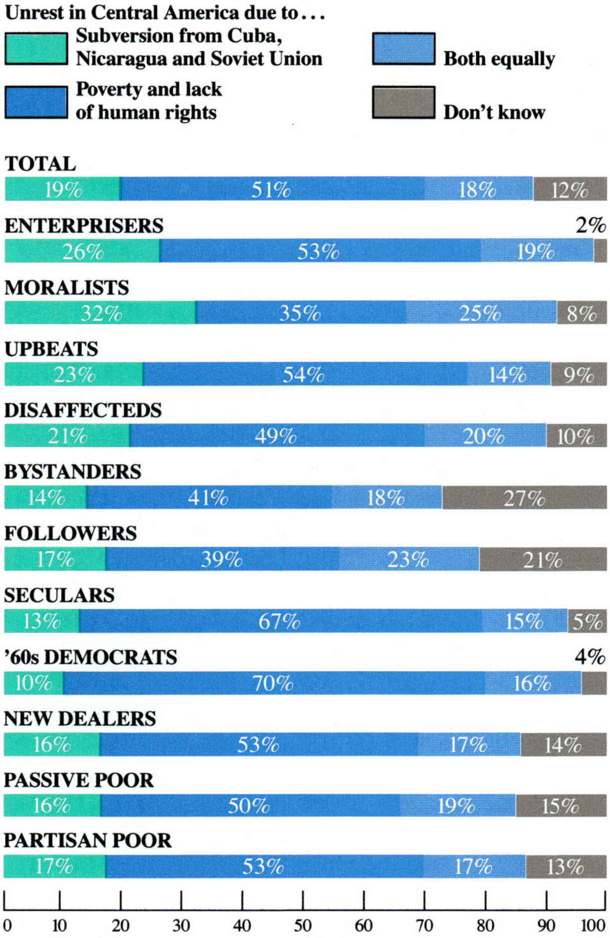

Unrest in Central America due to...

- Subversion from Cuba, Nicaragua and Soviet Union
- Poverty and lack of human rights
- Both equally
- Don't know

TOTAL
19% | 51% | 18% | 12%

ENTERPRISERS
2%
26% | 53% | 19%

MORALISTS
32% | 35% | 25% | 8%

UPBEATS
23% | 54% | 14% | 9%

DISAFFECTEDS
21% | 49% | 20% | 10%

BYSTANDERS
14% | 41% | 18% | 27%

FOLLOWERS
17% | 39% | 23% | 21%

SECULARS
13% | 67% | 15% | 5%

'60s DEMOCRATS
4%
10% | 70% | 16%

NEW DEALERS
16% | 53% | 17% | 14%

PASSIVE POOR
16% | 50% | 19% | 15%

PARTISAN POOR
17% | 53% | 17% | 13%

0   10   20   30   40   50   60   70   80   90   100

human rights cause the unrest. This is consistent with their partisan affiliation *and* their views on social justice. Interestingly, a rather high proportion of Upbeats also lean toward this position. Moralists (32 percent) are the strongest supporters of the Reagan policy in Central America. Although large numbers of Enterprisers say communist subversion (26 percent) causes the unrest, a significant proportion say poverty and lack of human rights (53 percent) are the cause. (*See Figure 16.*)

The Military

With Vietnam more than a decade behind us, Americans express a consensus in favor of the military—four out of five citizens (80 percent) rate the military very or mostly favorable. Considerably fewer Seculars (55 percent) and '60s Democrats (64 percent) rate the military favorably. However, when asked about the use of military force against terrorists that could risk civilian lives, an alliance emerges of the three groups most inclined to the use of force: Enterprisers (83 percent), Moralists (74 percent) and Disaffecteds (69 percent). Least likely to favor military force are the two most peace-oriented groups—'60s Democrats (46 percent) and Seculars (52 percent). (*See Figure 17.*)

FIGURE 17. ATTITUDES TOWARD THE MILITARY

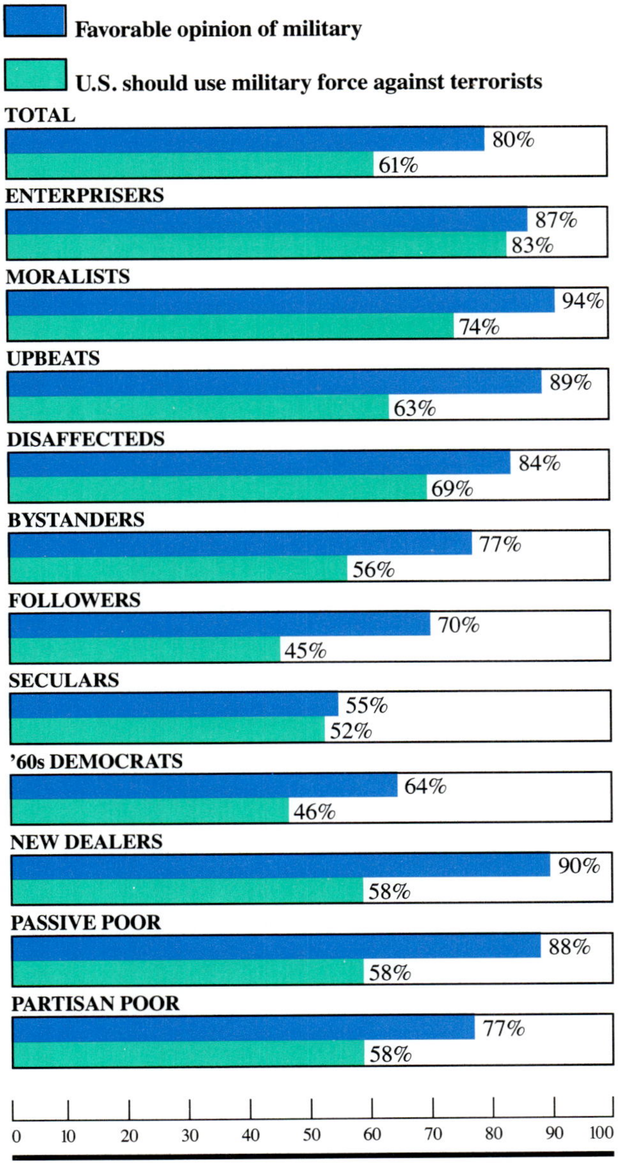

▇ **Favorable opinion of military**

▇ **U.S. should use military force against terrorists**

TOTAL
- 80%
- 61%

ENTERPRISERS
- 87%
- 83%

MORALISTS
- 94%
- 74%

UPBEATS
- 89%
- 63%

DISAFFECTEDS
- 84%
- 69%

BYSTANDERS
- 77%
- 56%

FOLLOWERS
- 70%
- 45%

SECULARS
- 55%
- 52%

'60s DEMOCRATS
- 64%
- 46%

NEW DEALERS
- 90%
- 58%

PASSIVE POOR
- 88%
- 58%

PARTISAN POOR
- 77%
- 58%

0 10 20 30 40 50 60 70 80 90 100

U.S. vs. U.S.S.R.

For the general population, opinion is divided almost equally on whether the United States or the Soviet Union is the stronger military power. (*See Figure 18.*)

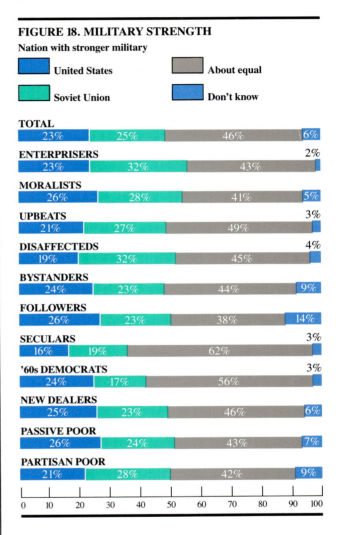

FIGURE 18. MILITARY STRENGTH

Nation with stronger military

▇ **United States**   ▇ **About equal**

▇ **Soviet Union**   ▇ **Don't know**

	United States	Soviet Union	About equal	Don't know
TOTAL	23%	25%	46%	6%
ENTERPRISERS	23%	32%	43%	2%
MORALISTS	26%	28%	41%	5%
UPBEATS	21%	27%	49%	3%
DISAFFECTEDS	19%	32%	45%	4%
BYSTANDERS	24%	23%	44%	9%
FOLLOWERS	26%	23%	38%	14%
SECULARS	16%	19%	62%	3%
'60s DEMOCRATS	24%	17%	56%	3%
NEW DEALERS	25%	23%	46%	6%
PASSIVE POOR	26%	24%	43%	7%
PARTISAN POOR	21%	28%	42%	9%

0 10 20 30 40 50 60 70 80 90 100

FIGURE 19. PEACE ISSUES

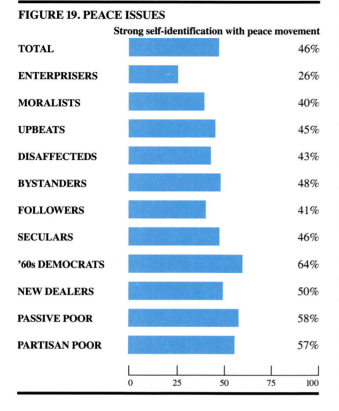

Strong self-identification with peace movement

TOTAL	46%
ENTERPRISERS	26%
MORALISTS	40%
UPBEATS	45%
DISAFFECTEDS	43%
BYSTANDERS	48%
FOLLOWERS	41%
SECULARS	46%
'60s DEMOCRATS	64%
NEW DEALERS	50%
PASSIVE POOR	58%
PARTISAN POOR	57%

Peace Issues

How to achieve world peace also divides the groups. The peace coalition emphasizes negotiation, arms reductions, a nuclear freeze and cuts in defense spending. The anti-communist/pro-strong defense alliance is suspicious of other countries and stresses the need for a strong defense as the cornerstone for maintaining peace. In contrast, about two-thirds of the '60s Democrats (64 percent) strongly self-identify themselves as supporters of the peace movement. Also higher than average are the Passive Poor (58 percent) and Partisan Poor (57 percent). Enterprisers (26 percent) are least likely to strongly self-identify as a supporter of the peace movement. (*See Figure 19.*)

Defense Spending

Fewer than one American in four (24 percent) feels that defense spending should be increased. Moralists (37 percent) and, to a small degree, Passive Poor (31 percent) are the only typology groups that favor increasing the defense budget in higher proportions. When respondents were asked whether they favored or opposed cutting

back federal spending for defense, Enterprisers (31 percent) join Moralists (31 percent) in being least likely to support that idea. Sixties Democrats (69 percent) and Seculars (68 percent) are the most likely to agree to defense cuts. (*See Figure 20.*)

FIGURE 20. DEFENSE SPENDING

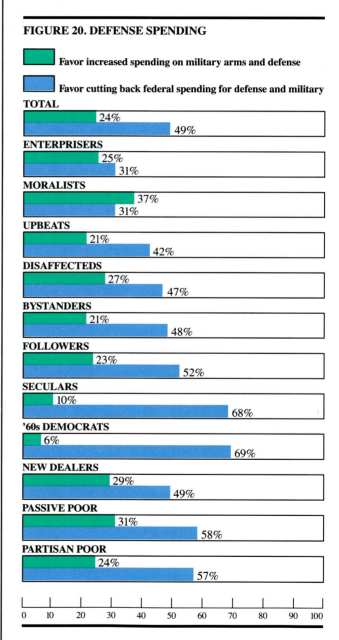

Favor increased spending on military arms and defense

Favor cutting back federal spending for defense and military

TOTAL	24%	49%
ENTERPRISERS	25%	31%
MORALISTS	37%	31%
UPBEATS	21%	42%
DISAFFECTEDS	27%	47%
BYSTANDERS	21%	48%
FOLLOWERS	23%	52%
SECULARS	10%	68%
'60s DEMOCRATS	6%	69%
NEW DEALERS	29%	49%
PASSIVE POOR	31%	58%
PARTISAN POOR	24%	57%

FIGURE 21. "STAR WARS"

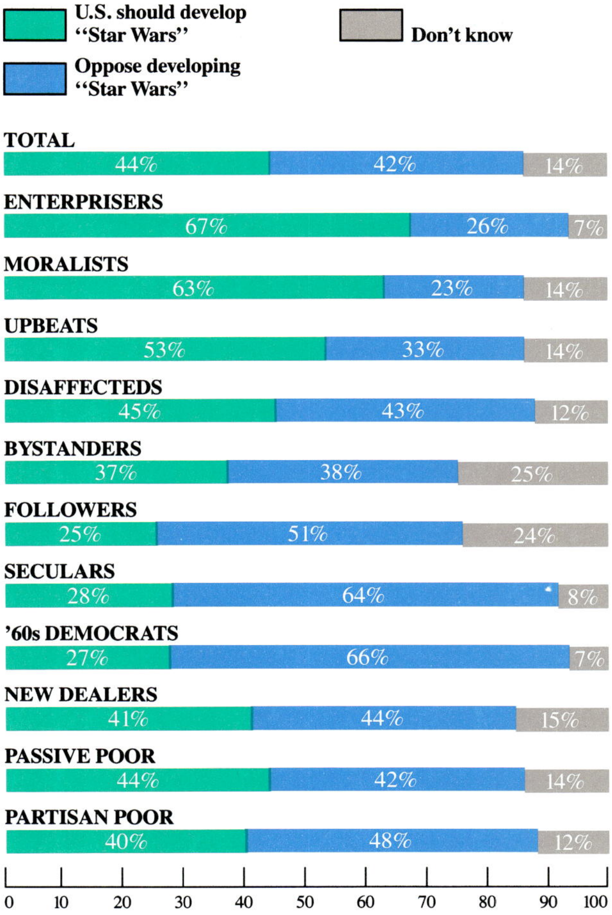

■ U.S. should develop "Star Wars"   ■ Don't know
■ Oppose developing "Star Wars"

Group	Develop	Oppose	Don't know
TOTAL	44%	42%	14%
ENTERPRISERS	67%	26%	7%
MORALISTS	63%	23%	14%
UPBEATS	53%	33%	14%
DISAFFECTEDS	45%	43%	12%
BYSTANDERS	37%	38%	25%
FOLLOWERS	25%	51%	24%
SECULARS	28%	64%	8%
'60s DEMOCRATS	27%	66%	7%
NEW DEALERS	41%	44%	15%
PASSIVE POOR	44%	42%	14%
PARTISAN POOR	40%	48%	12%

0 10 20 30 40 50 60 70 80 90 100

"Star Wars"

Expensive boondoggle or ultimate solution for world peace—that's how most people divide on the question of the Strategic Defense Initiative (SDI), or "Star Wars." Sixties Democrats and the Seculars lead the peace-oriented coalition with nearly two-thirds opposing "Star Wars." The pro-SDI groups are Enterprisers (67 percent), Moralists (63 percent) and to a lesser degree Upbeats (53 percent). (*See Figure 21.*)

Arms Negotiations

Three questions explored strategies for nuclear arms reductions. The position of the '60s Democrats and Seculars is one of being more willing to trust the Russians, compromising if necessary and being less concerned about falling behind in nuclear weaponry. They stand apart from all the other groups in feeling that the United States is not willing enough to compromise with the Soviet Union.

An equally solid bloc of Enterprisers and Moralists believe trusting the Russians to live up to an arms agreement is the greater risk to peace. (*See Figure 22.*)

FIGURE 22. ARMS NEGOTIATIONS

	TOTAL	ENTERPRISERS	MORALISTS	UPBEATS	DISAFFECTEDS	BYSTANDERS	FOLLOWERS	SECULARS	'60s DEMOCRATS	NEW DEALERS	PASSIVE POOR	PARTISAN POOR
To reduce tensions with the Soviet Union, U.S. policy...												
Too willing to compromise	22%	25%	26%	24%	26%	22%	20%	12%	12%	25%	25%	29%
Not willing enough to compromise	23%	12%	10%	20%	24%	20%	23%	44%	43%	19%	20%	26%
About right	46%	60%	58%	52%	45%	41%	38%	38%	41%	46%	43%	34%
Don't know	9%	3%	6%	4%	5%	17%	19%	6%	4%	10%	12%	11%
	100%	100%	100%	100%	100%	100%	100%	100%	100%	100%	100%	100%
Chances of nuclear war increased with...												
Continuation of arms buildup	42%	32%	31%	43%	40%	37%	36%	65%	69%	34%	39%	43%
U.S. falling behind Soviet Union in nuclear weaponry	41%	56%	53%	43%	47%	36%	31%	25%	22%	48%	42%	42%
Don't know	17%	12%	16%	14%	13%	27%	33%	10%	9%	18%	19%	15%
	100%	100%	100%	100%	100%	100%	100%	100%	100%	100%	100%	100%
Greater risk to peace...												
Trusting Russians to live up to their side of an arms agreement	43%	51%	57%	45%	48%	38%	38%	28%	30%	46%	37%	42%
Being too suspicious of Russians so we never get an agreement	41%	40%	30%	41%	37%	36%	34%	62%	61%	38%	42%	39%
Can't say/ don't know	16%	9%	13%	14%	15%	26%	28%	10%	9%	16%	21%	19%
	100%	100%	100%	100%	100%	100%	100%	100%	100%	100%	100%	100%

FIGURE 23. TRADE POLICIES

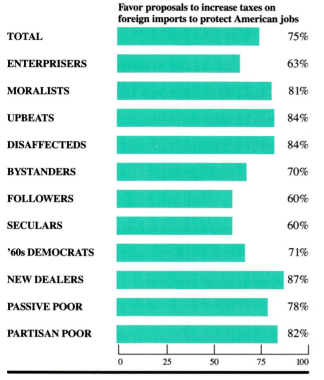

Favor proposals to increase taxes on foreign imports to protect American jobs

TOTAL	75%
ENTERPRISERS	63%
MORALISTS	81%
UPBEATS	84%
DISAFFECTEDS	84%
BYSTANDERS	70%
FOLLOWERS	60%
SECULARS	60%
'60s DEMOCRATS	71%
NEW DEALERS	87%
PASSIVE POOR	78%
PARTISAN POOR	82%

Trade Policies

A very different alliance of groups emerges when foreign policy shifts from defense to economic policy. Because New Dealers are most likely to live in a labor union household, they lead the coalition favoring protectionist proposals to increase taxes on foreign imports to save American jobs (87 percent). Given the New Dealers' large impact in Democratic primaries, one can understand Congressman Richard Gephardt's strategy in emphasizing tough trade measures in his presidential campaign. (*See Figure 23.*)

FIGURE 24. SCALOMETER RATINGS OF COUNTRIES—"TOTAL FAVORABLE RATINGS"*

	TOTAL	ENTERPRISERS	MORALISTS	UPBEATS	DISAFFECTEDS	BYSTANDERS	FOLLOWERS	SECULARS	'60s DEMOCRATS	NEW DEALERS	PASSIVE POOR	PARTISAN POOR
Canada	93%	97%	97%	97%	96%	87%	87%	98%	97%	95%	87%	88%
Great Britain	88%	97%	93%	95%	93%	80%	86%	91%	96%	86%	74%	80%
West Germany	75%	92%	80%	81%	71%	61%	64%	90%	84%	68%	62%	70%
Japan	69%	81%	68%	81%	61%	66%	58%	84%	77%	56%	65%	62%
Mexico	67%	66%	61%	73%	62%	70%	72%	66%	76%	65%	64%	61%
Israel	65%	72%	68%	69%	67%	55%	63%	72%	71%	68%	56%	54%
China	65%	71%	64%	72%	58%	56%	62%	74%	81%	54%	59%	62%
South Africa	29%	31%	35%	30%	26%	33%	36%	17%	16%	32%	31%	29%
Soviet Union	25%	27%	14%	31%	14%	22%	21%	44%	46%	16%	24%	20%
Iran	7%	2%	5%	5%	5%	8%	16%	4%	9%	8%	14%	8%

*Total favorable ratings = score of +1 through +5, on a scale from −5 to +5.

Rating Foreign Countries

Americans consider Canadians their best friends and Iranians their worst enemies among the 10 countries rated for general favorability. The Soviet Union and South Africa also receive strong unfavorable ratings. (*See Figure 24.*)

The most interesting finding in the group ratings of the 10 countries is a comparison between South Africa and the Soviet Union. Overall, one-fourth rate the Soviet Union (25 percent) favorably, and slightly more rate South Africa (29 percent) favorably. However, the percentage of anti-communist and racially intolerant Moralists and New Dealers who rate South Africa favorably is more than twice as large as the percentage who rate the Soviet Union favorably. Disaffecteds also rate South Africa favorably in significantly higher numbers than they do the Soviet Union—as do the Partisan Poor, Passive Poor and Followers. These groups are the most likely to be composed of politically unsophisticated people who do not follow world affairs. Racially tolerant and peace-oriented '60s Democrats and Seculars, on the other hand, rate the Soviet Union favorably in percentages nearly four times larger than they do South Africa.

POSITIONS ON OTHER ISSUES
Environment

Sixties Democrats (76 percent) and Seculars (71 percent) are most likely to support increased federal funding to improve and protect the environment, while Enterprisers (44 percent) are least likely to do so. However, when the question narrows to relaxing environmental controls to allow economic growth, job-conscious Passive Poor, Partisan Poor, New Dealers, Followers and Moralists leap to the top of the groups favoring such a proposal. (*See Figure 25.*)

FIGURE 25. POSITIONS ON OTHER ISSUES

Environment

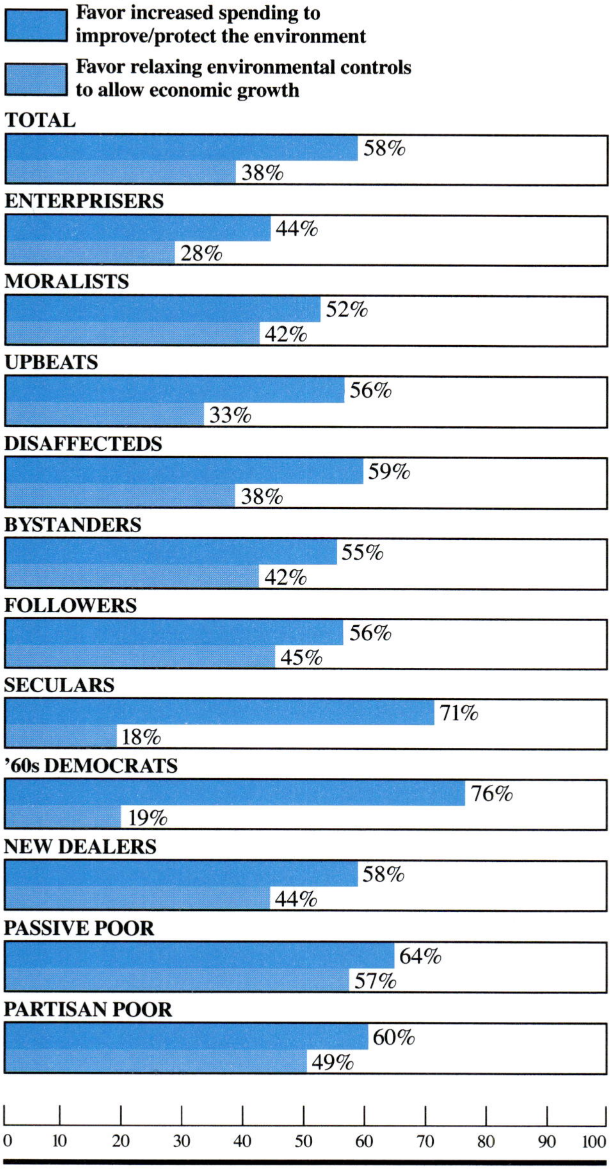

Favor increased spending to
improve/protect the environment

Favor relaxing environmental controls
to allow economic growth

TOTAL
58%
38%

ENTERPRISERS
44%
28%

MORALISTS
52%
42%

UPBEATS
56%
33%

DISAFFECTEDS
59%
38%

BYSTANDERS
55%
42%

FOLLOWERS
56%
45%

SECULARS
71%
18%

'60s DEMOCRATS
76%
19%

NEW DEALERS
58%
44%

PASSIVE POOR
64%
57%

PARTISAN POOR
60%
49%

0 10 20 30 40 50 60 70 80 90 100

FIGURE 25 (cont.) POSITIONS ON OTHER ISSUES

Death penalty

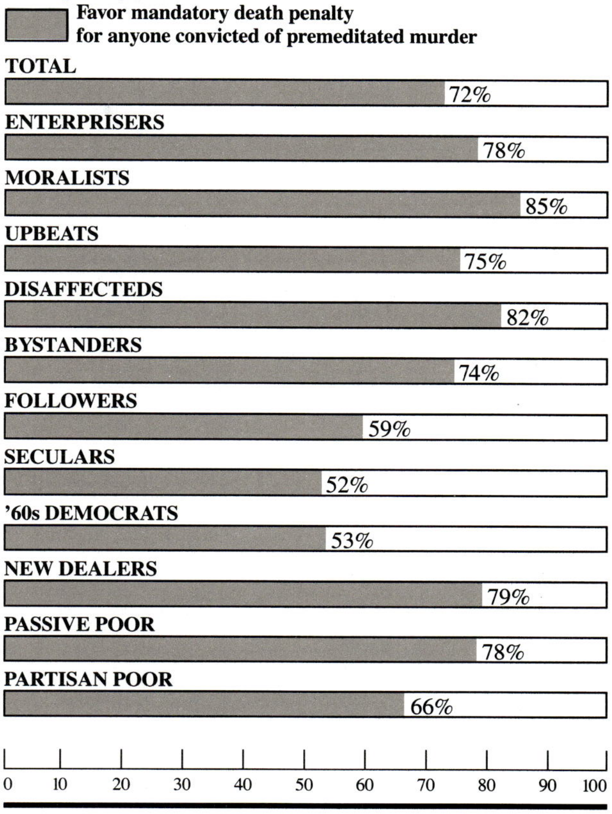

Favor mandatory death penalty
for anyone convicted of premeditated murder

TOTAL
72%

ENTERPRISERS
78%

MORALISTS
85%

UPBEATS
75%

DISAFFECTEDS
82%

BYSTANDERS
74%

FOLLOWERS
59%

SECULARS
52%

'60s DEMOCRATS
53%

NEW DEALERS
79%

PASSIVE POOR
78%

PARTISAN POOR
66%

0 10 20 30 40 50 60 70 80 90 100

FIGURE 25 (cont.) POSITIONS ON OTHER ISSUES

Education

■ Favor increased spending on improving the nation's public schools

□ Favor increased spending on financial aid for college students

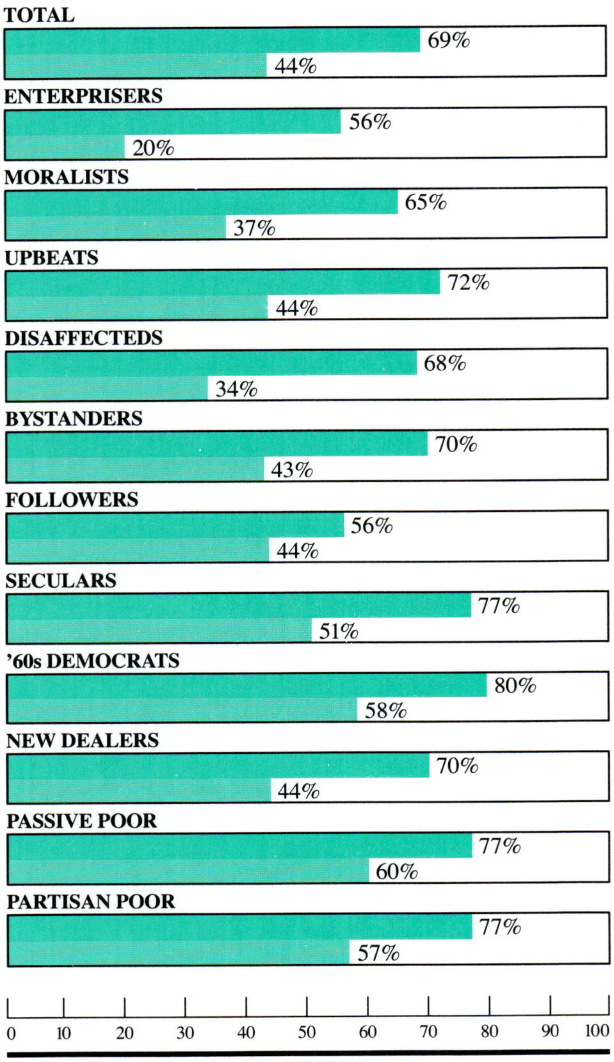

TOTAL
69%
44%

ENTERPRISERS
56%
20%

MORALISTS
65%
37%

UPBEATS
72%
44%

DISAFFECTEDS
68%
34%

BYSTANDERS
70%
43%

FOLLOWERS
56%
44%

SECULARS
77%
51%

'60s DEMOCRATS
80%
58%

NEW DEALERS
70%
44%

PASSIVE POOR
77%
60%

PARTISAN POOR
77%
57%

0 10 20 30 40 50 60 70 80 90 100

FIGURE 25 (cont.) POSITIONS ON OTHER ISSUES

Taxes

■ Oppose proposals to increase taxes to reduce federal budget deficit

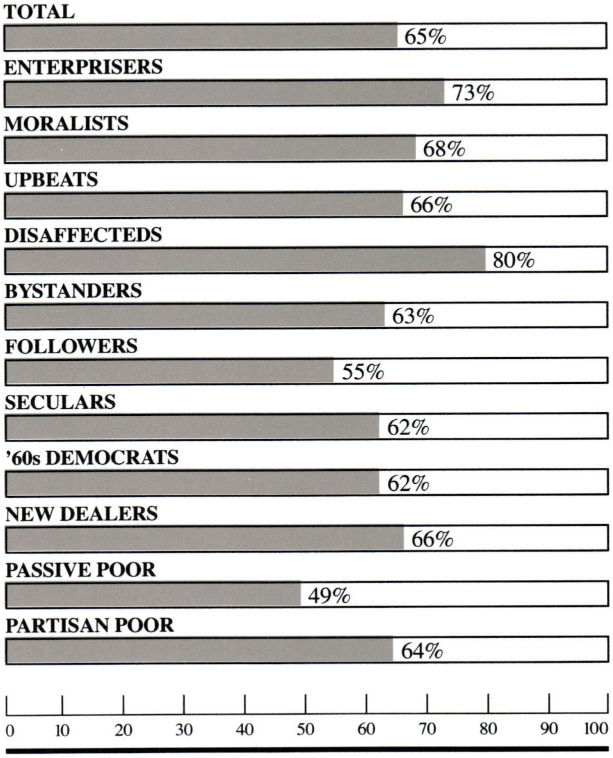

TOTAL
65%

ENTERPRISERS
73%

MORALISTS
68%

UPBEATS
66%

DISAFFECTEDS
80%

BYSTANDERS
63%

FOLLOWERS
55%

SECULARS
62%

'60s DEMOCRATS
62%

NEW DEALERS
66%

PASSIVE POOR
49%

PARTISAN POOR
64%

0 10 20 30 40 50 60 70 80 90 100

Death Penalty

A different alignment is seen on the issue of a mandatory death penalty for anyone convicted of murder. Intolerance for criminals pushes the Moralists to the top of the pro-death penalty coalition. Sixties Democrats and the Seculars are much more likely to view crime as a social problem, rather than a moral one; these groups emerge as strong opponents of the death penalty.

Education

Seven in 10 Americans favor increasing federal spending to improve the nation's public school systems. Sixties Democrats (80 percent), Seculars (77 percent), Passive Poor (77 percent) and the Partisan Poor (77 percent) favor this proposition most strongly. Even a majority of Enterprisers (56 percent) favor such an increase, although they are the group least likely to support this measure.

Opinion is divided on the issue of financial aid to college students. Upper-middle class '60s Democrats (58 percent), the Partisan Poor (57 percent) and Passive Poor (60 percent) all favor increased financial aid for college students in higher than average numbers.

Taxes

In a response that will make President Reagan's day, Americans oppose (65 percent) federal income tax increases to reduce the federal deficit. Enterprisers (73 percent) and Disaffecteds (80 percent) are most likely to oppose income tax increases. The Passive Poor (49 percent) are the least likely to oppose the tax increase.

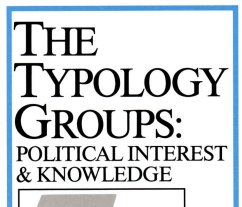

THE TYPOLOGY GROUPS:
POLITICAL INTEREST & KNOWLEDGE

7

Seventy-six percent of the American people say they pay attention to government and public affairs: '60s Democrats (59 percent), Enterprisers (59 percent) and Seculars (55 percent) are the most attentive. (*See Figure 26.*)

We asked three questions to test knowledge of public affairs: Which side does the U.S. support in Nicaragua? Has the federal budget deficit increased, decreased or stayed about the same in the past five years? Who is the White House chief of staff (all names on the list were past or the current chief of staff)?

About three-quarters of the population know that the federal budget deficit has increased over the past five years. Nine out of 10 Enterprisers (90 percent), Seculars (90 percent) and '60s Democrats (87 percent) give the correct answer. Followers (44 percent), Bystanders (53 percent) and Passive Poor (58 percent) are least likely to know the right answer.

FIGURE 26. POLITICAL INTEREST

Follow what goes on in government and public affairs

- Most of the time
- Only now and then
- Don't know
- Some of the time
- Hardly at all

TOTAL — 41% | 35% | 15% | 7% | 2%

ENTERPRISERS — 59% | 32% | 6% | 2% 1%

MORALISTS — 48% | 38% | 9% | 3% 2%

UPBEATS — 39% | 47% | 11% | 3% *

DISAFFECTEDS — 41% | 35% | 20% | 3% 1%

BYSTANDERS — 11% | 21% | 32% | 33% | 3%

FOLLOWERS — 23% | 39% | 20% | 12% | 6%

SECULARS — 55% | 33% | 8% | 2% 2%

'60s DEMOCRATS — 59% | 30% | 10% | 1% *

NEW DEALERS — 45% | 39% | 11% | 4% 1%

PASSIVE POOR — 35% | 35% | 19% | 10% | 1%

PARTISAN POOR — 37% | 36% | 18% | 7% | 2%

0 10 20 30 40 50 60 70 80 90 100

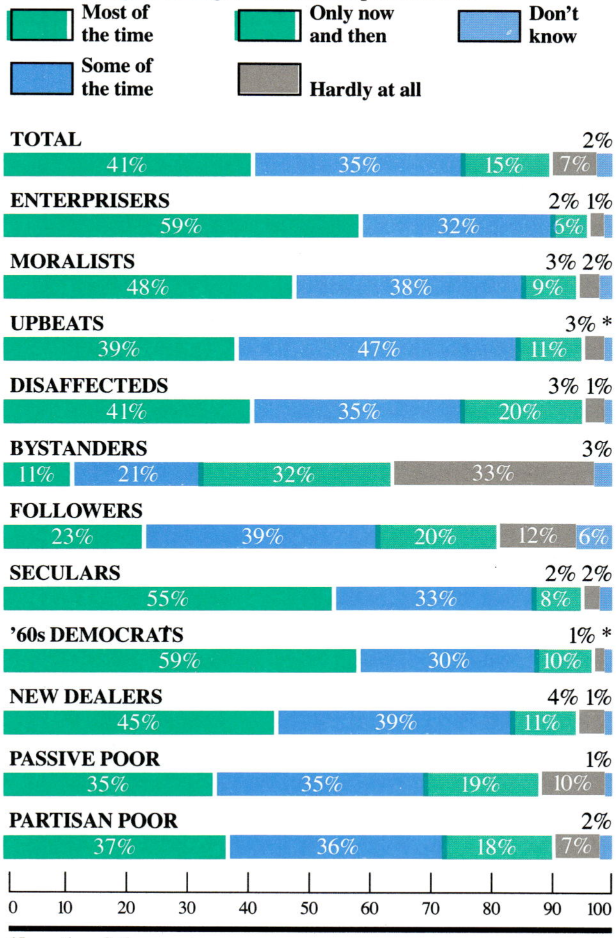

*Less than 0.5 percent.

One out of two Americans surveyed (49 percent) know that Howard Baker is the White House Chief of Staff. Again, high proportions of the three politically sophisticated groups gave the correct answer: Seculars (70 percent), Enterprisers (68 percent) and '60s Democrats (64 percent).

Only a plurality know the United States backs those opposing the government in Nicaragua (45 percent), and nearly two in five Americans volunteer that they are not sure or don't know (39 percent). Interestingly, three of the more anti-communist and militaristic groups—Moralists, Passive Poor and New Dealers—have average or below-average knowledge about the Nicaraguan situation. (These may have been the groups most influenced by Lt. Col. Oliver North's testimony regarding Nicaragua.)

These three questions were combined into a knowledge scale ranging from zero (missed all three questions) to three (all answers correct). Twenty-six percent of the general population scores high (three out of three); 32 percent get two in three right; and 42 percent score low by giving only one or no correct answers. So going back to our first question, while 76 percent of the people *say* they pay attention to politics, they clearly aren't taking notes.

Overall, the three most knowledgeable groups remain the Seculars (53 percent), '60s Democrats (46 percent) and Enterprisers (44 percent), since high proportions of the members in these groups know the right answer to all three questions. Bystanders, Followers, Passive Poor and the Partisan Poor are the least informed typology groups. (*See Figures 27 and 28.*)

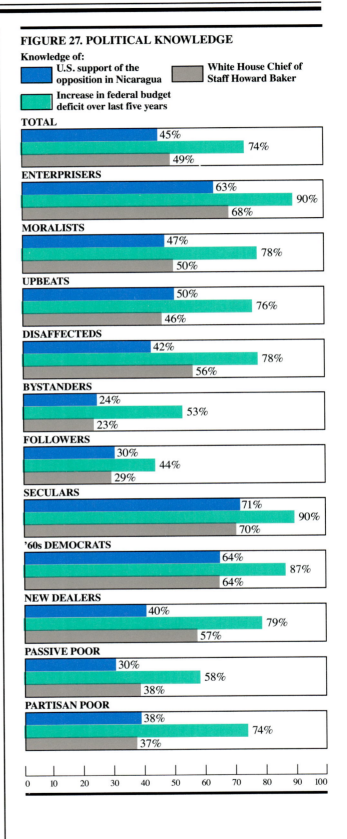

FIGURE 27. POLITICAL KNOWLEDGE

Knowledge of:
- U.S. support of the opposition in Nicaragua
- White House Chief of Staff Howard Baker
- Increase in federal budget deficit over last five years

TOTAL
45% / 74% / 49%

ENTERPRISERS
63% / 90% / 68%

MORALISTS
47% / 78% / 50%

UPBEATS
50% / 76% / 46%

DISAFFECTEDS
42% / 78% / 56%

BYSTANDERS
24% / 53% / 23%

FOLLOWERS
30% / 44% / 29%

SECULARS
71% / 90% / 70%

'60s DEMOCRATS
64% / 87% / 64%

NEW DEALERS
40% / 79% / 57%

PASSIVE POOR
30% / 58% / 38%

PARTISAN POOR
38% / 74% / 37%

0 10 20 30 40 50 60 70 80 90 100

FIGURE 28. KNOWLEDGE SCALE

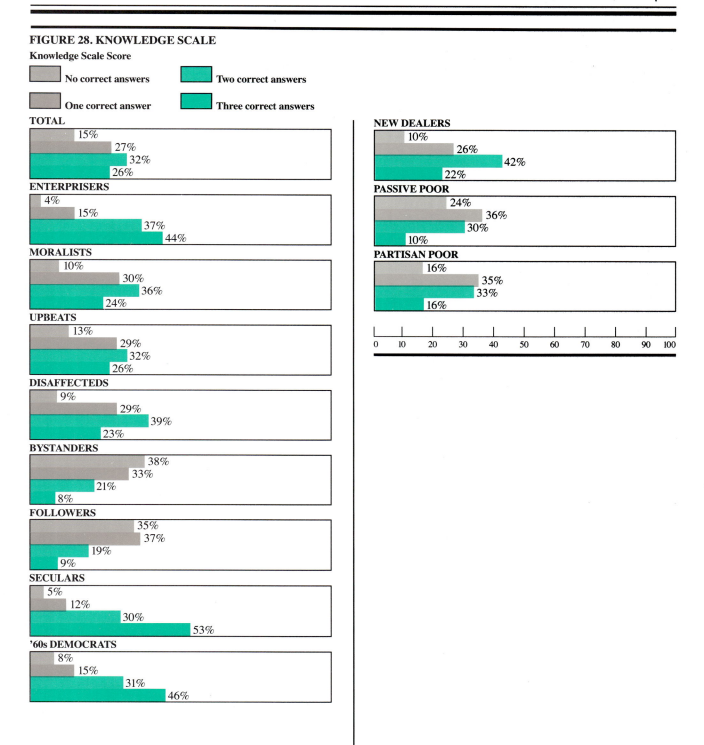

Knowledge Scale Score

- No correct answers
- One correct answer
- Two correct answers
- Three correct answers

TOTAL
- 15%
- 27%
- 32%
- 26%

ENTERPRISERS
- 4%
- 15%
- 37%
- 44%

MORALISTS
- 10%
- 30%
- 36%
- 24%

UPBEATS
- 13%
- 29%
- 32%
- 26%

DISAFFECTEDS
- 9%
- 29%
- 39%
- 23%

BYSTANDERS
- 38%
- 33%
- 21%
- 8%

FOLLOWERS
- 35%
- 37%
- 19%
- 9%

SECULARS
- 5%
- 12%
- 30%
- 53%

'60s DEMOCRATS
- 8%
- 15%
- 31%
- 46%

NEW DEALERS
- 10%
- 26%
- 42%
- 22%

PASSIVE POOR
- 24%
- 36%
- 30%
- 10%

PARTISAN POOR
- 16%
- 35%
- 33%
- 16%

0 10 20 30 40 50 60 70 80 90 100

THE TYPOLOGY GROUPS:
POLITICAL INVOLVEMENT

8

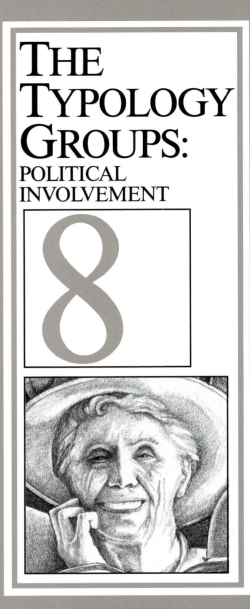

In nonvoting political activities, Enterprisers, '60s Democrats and Seculars are most likely to sign petitions, join organizations in support of a cause and attend public hearings. Seculars, '60s Democrats and to a lesser extent Enterprisers are most likely to boycott a company. Disaffecteds (64 percent) and to a lesser extent Upbeats (59 percent) are heavy petition signers. (*See Figures 29 and 30.*)

FIGURE 29. INCIDENCE OF NONVOTING POLITICAL ACTIVITIES

| | TOTAL | Republican clusters | | | | |
		ENTERPRISERS	MORALISTS	UPBEATS	DISAFFECTEDS	BYSTANDERS
Response						
Signed a petition	55%	79%	55%	59%	64%	26%
Wrote letter, telephoned, sent telegram to editor, public official or company	30%	50%	28%	33%	30%	12%
Attended public hearing or meeting of special-interest organization	23%	34%	22%	25%	23%	7%
Contacted representative to U.S. House of Representatives	21%	42%	25%	21%	22%	3%
Contacted U.S. senator	19%	36%	24%	18%	20%	2%
Joined organization in support of particular cause	17%	25%	15%	19%	13%	8%
Boycotted company	14%	20%	14%	15%	16%	3%
Spoke at public hearing or forum	6%	10%	4%	5%	4%	1%

FIGURE 30. INCIDENCE OF NONVOTING POLITICAL ACTIVITIES

			Democratic clusters			
	FOLLOWERS	SECULARS	'60s DEMOCRATS	NEW DEALERS	PASSIVE POOR	PARTISAN POOR
Response						
Signed petition	35%	73%	76%	51%	36%	49%
Wrote letter, telephoned, sent telegram to editor, public official or company	17%	40%	53%	24%	20%	19%
Attended public hearing or meeting of special-interest organization	14%	33%	40%	20%	17%	20%
Contacted representative to U.S. House of Representatives	10%	25%	36%	22%	10%	15%
Contacted U.S. senator	8%	23%	31%	22%	12%	14%
Joined organization in support of particular cause	8%	27%	37%	11%	9%	16%
Boycotted company	4%	28%	30%	9%	6%	16%
Spoke at public hearing or forum	1%	7%	15%	6%	4%	5%

Contributions to candidates, political parties and PACs among the general population provide an assessment of the inter-party competition for campaign dollars. Members of the Republican and lean Republican groups are more likely than those in the Democratic groups to contribute money to political *candidates* (51 percent vs. 48 percent) and to their *political party* (54 percent vs. 44 percent), while members of the Democratic groups are more likely than the Republicans to contribute to *PAC*s (53 percent vs. 45 percent).

The two solidly Republican clusters account for two in five of all contributions to political parties. Enterprisers (24 percent) make up the largest single group of financial contributors to political parties, and the Moralists (16 percent) are the second largest group. By comparison, the four solidly Democratic groups, combined, only account for one-third (32 percent) of the financial contributors to political parties. Though it is true that the Democratic groups are disproportionately composed of the less affluent and poor, the proportion of givers from the '60s Democrats is roughly half that of the Enterprisers and

five percentage points lower than the Moralists. When the independent groups are added to the calculation based on their partisan leaning, Republican domination in the area of the financial contributions to their political party is made even more dramatic (54 percent vs. 44 percent).

The pattern of partisan support is reversed in the instance of *working* for a political party or candidate and for financial contributions to PACs. The solid Democratic groups (42 percent) make up more than two out of five political workers in the general population compared with three in 10 among the solid GOP segments (30 percent).

The proportions who contribute to PACs among the Democratic groups exceed that of the Republicans (53 percent vs. 45 percent). Enterprisers account for 18 percent of the contributions to PACs. (*See Figure 31.*)

FIGURE 31. CAMPAIGN CONTRIBUTORS AND POLITICAL PARTY WORKERS

	Total	Contributed money to			Worked for party
		Candidate	PACs	Party	
Solid Republican groups					
Enterprisers	10%	23%	18%	24%	16%
Moralists	11%	12%	10%	16%	14%
	21%	35%	28%	40%	30%
Independent groups leaning Republican					
Upbeats	9%	9%	10%	7%	7%
Disaffecteds	9%	7%	7%	7%	7%
	18%	16%	17%	14%	14%
Independent groups leaning Democratic					
Followers	7%	4%	3%	4%	5%
Seculars	8%	10%	12%	8%	7%
	15%	14%	15%	12%	12%
Solid Democratic groups					
'60s Democrats	8%	14%	16%	11%	14%
New Dealers	11%	11%	11%	11%	12%
Passive Poor	7%	3%	5%	5%	6%
Partisan Poor	9%	6%	6%	5%	10%
	35%	34%	38%	32%	42%
Bystanders (noninvolved)	11%	1%	2%	2%	2%

"Enterprisers make up the largest single group of financial contributors to political parties..."

THE TYPOLOGY GROUPS: MEDIA HABITS

9

While two-thirds of the population report that they read the newspaper every day (66 percent), a larger proportion watch network television evening news regularly (72 percent). Television watching and newspaper readership are related to education and interest in politics, a finding that is reflected by responses across typology groups on their media usage habits. Significantly higher proportions of Enterprisers, '60s Democrats and Seculars read newspapers every day. (*See Figure 32.*)

More than one-quarter of the public rely most on their daily newspapers (28 percent) for information on national affairs, while more than one-half of the population rely most on television (56 percent) for national affairs information, and another one in 10 say radio (9 percent). Those who rely on newspapers, in contrast to those who rely on television for providing information on national affairs, are better educated, possess a higher level of interest and involvement in politics and are more likely to vote. (*See Figure 33.*)

FIGURE 32. MEDIA USE

	Reads newspaper regularly	Watches TV network news regularly
Total	66%	72%
Solid Republican groups		
Enterprisers	75%	63%
Moralists	74%	78%
Independent groups leaning Republican		
Upbeats	65%	65%
Disaffecteds	63%	71%
Independent groups leaning Democratic		
Followers	63%	68%
Seculars	74%	64%
Solid Democratic groups		
'60s Democrats	75%	68%
New Dealers	75%	84%
Passive Poor	64%	83%
Partisan Poor	54%	82%
Bystanders (noninvolved)	45%	62%

FIGURE 33. RELIANCE ON NEWSPAPERS VS. TELEVISION BY KEY INDICATORS

	Total	Rely most on newspapers	Rely most on television
Education			
Any college	36%	49%	28%
No college	64%	51%	72%
Highest political knowledge	26%	35%	21%
Follow government and public affairs most of the time	41%	50%	38%
Most likely to vote	49%	55%	47%
Partisan actions Contributed money to...			
Candidate	15%	20%	11%
Party	12%	14%	10%
PAC	12%	16%	9%
Worked for party	11%	13%	10%
Nonpartisan actions			
Signed a petition	55%	65%	50%
Joined organization in support of cause	17%	20%	14%
Spoke at public hearing or forum	6%	7%	4%

"More than one-quarter of the public rely most on their daily newspapers for information on national affairs..."

The largest difference between people who rely on newspapers versus those who rely on television is found on beliefs about Tolerance. A larger proportion of those who rely on television (29 percent) hold highly intolerant views, compared with those who rely most on newspapers (19 percent). In addition, one in four of the population who rely on television (25 percent) score high on the Religious Faith scale, while only one in five of those who most rely on newspapers are highly religious. Members of the public who demonstrate high levels of political alienation rely most on television (27 percent) in significantly greater proportions than those who rely on newspapers (21 percent).

Because of these relationships among political values and reliance on television compared with newspapers for information about public affairs, opinions on several contemporary issues vary somewhat between these two groups. Specifically, those who rely most on newspapers are less likely to favor increased spending for social welfare programs, such as programs for the homeless or elderly; are less likely to favor drug tests or making it more difficult for a woman to get an abortion; are somewhat less likely to favor an import tax to protect jobs, the death penalty, limiting the access AIDS patients have to public places or relaxing environmental controls for economic growth and development. (*See Figure 34.*)

FIGURE 34. OPINIONS ON ISSUES

	Total	Rely most on newspaper	Rely most on television
Favor import tax to protect American jobs	75%	72%	79%
Favor death penalty	72%	70%	75%
Favor increased spending on programs for the homeless	68%	64%	71%
Favor increased spending on programs for the elderly	75%	70%	79%
Favor mandatory drug tests	65%	59%	70%
Favor ''Star Wars''	52%	50%	53%
Favor cutbacks in defense spending	49%	50%	50%
Favor limiting access of AIDS patients to public places	44%	38%	42%
Favor making it more difficult for woman to get abortion	41%	37%	44%
Favor relaxing environmental controls to allow growth and development	38%	33%	41%
Favor increased spending on aid to the Contras	9%	9%	9%

FIGURE 35. PRINT VS. TELEVISION

	Total	Rely most on newspapers	Rely most on television
Solid Republican groups			
Enterprisers	10%	13%	7%
Moralists	11%	12%	11%
	21%	25%	18%
Independent groups leaning Republican			
Upbeats	9%	10%	9%
Disaffecteds	9%	9%	8%
	18%	19%	17%
Independent groups leaning Democratic			
Followers	7%	7%	7%
Seculars	8%	13%	5%
	15%	20%	12%
Solid Democratic groups			
'60s Democrats	8%	11%	7%
New Dealers	11%	9%	14%
Passive Poor	7%	5%	9%
Partisan Poor	9%	5%	11%
	35%	30%	41%
Bystanders (noninvolved)	11%	6%	12%

Media preferences for information about public affairs differ across the typology groups, primarily by political sophistication. Compared with the general population, Republicans are more likely to rely on newspapers. A greater proportion of members from the Democratic groups, compared to the Republican groups, rely most on television for information on public affairs (53 percent vs. 35 percent). More specifically, the groups that rely most on television are the more religious, less tolerant New Dealers (14 percent) and Moralists (11 percent), as well as the Partisan Poor (11 percent). (*See Figure 35.*)

THE ROLE OF TELEVISION COMMERCIALS

Several survey questions explore the role of political television commercials. One out of two members of the public report that they do not become aware of political candidates until they see their advertising on television. Among those that do, the largest numbers are groups that are solid or lean to the Democratic Party (47 percent), while about two in five (39 percent) are core Republicans or GOP leaners. Together Moralists and New Dealers make up one-quarter (25 percent) of those who first become aware of candidates from television ads. The more upscale, politically sophisticated Enterprisers, '60s Democrats and Seculars are least likely to first learn of candidates through TV ads—only 17 percent.

Nearly three in five Americans (57 percent) get "some sense of what a candidate is like" through candidates' television commercials. Equal proportions of Democratic and Republican group members and leaners are found among those who at least mostly agree with that statement (40 percent vs. 39 percent). Again, New Dealers (14 percent) and Moralists (12 percent) make up the largest bloc among those who say that they get some sense of what a candidate is like through their television commercials.

The distribution of percentages across the typology groups changes when respondents were asked if they liked to have a picture of a candidate in their mind when going to vote for him or her. While this question does not specify candidate commercials, seven out of 10 Americans (70 percent) completely or mostly agree with the statement. (*See Figure 36.*)

FIGURE 36. POLITICAL ADVERTISING ON TELEVISION

	Agree completely or mostly		
	Become aware of candidates through TV commercials	Get sense of what candidate is like through TV commercials	Like to have picture of candidate in mind when voting
Solid Republican groups			
Enterprisers	8%	9%	12%
Moralists	11%	12%	12%
	19%	21%	24%
Independent groups leaning Republican			
Upbeats	9%	9%	11%
Disaffecteds	11%	9%	9%
	20%	18%	20%
Independent groups leaning Democratic			
Followers	6%	6%	6%
Seculars	5%	6%	7%
	11%	12%	13%
Solid Democratic groups			
'60s Democrats	4%	6%	8%
New Dealers	14%	14%	13%
Passive Poor	8%	7%	6%
Partisan Poor	10%	11%	9%
	36%	38%	36%
Bystanders (noninvolved)	14%	11%	7%

Respondents were asked to choose between news reports on television versus candidates' television commercials as the one that gives a better idea of "what a candidate is like personally" and "where a candidate stands on issues." About one-quarter of the public preferred commercials for giving a better idea of what a candidate is like personally, and a smaller 14 percent said commercials give a better idea of where a candidate stands on the issues. There are no differences in the distribution of responses to these questions among the typology groups. (*See Figure 37.*)

FIGURE 37. TELEVISION COMMERCIALS VS. NEWS REPORTS

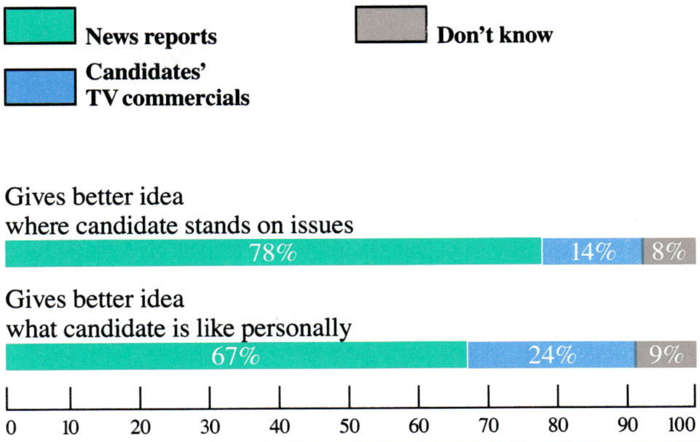

■ News reports   ■ Don't know
■ Candidates'
TV commercials

Gives better idea
where candidate stands on issues
78%   14%   8%

Gives better idea
what candidate is like personally
67%   24%   9%

0 10 20 30 40 50 60 70 80 90 100

THE TYPOLOGY GROUPS:

SOCIOECONOMIC STATUS & LIFESTYLE

10

Socioeconomic status is measured by education, income and occupation. Three familiar groups are at the top of the socioeconomic ladder: Enterprisers, Seculars and '60s Democrats. Each of these groups is more highly educated (at least 40 percent have college degrees), has higher incomes and is primarily white-collar.

At the lowest end are the Bystanders, the Partisan Poor, Followers and Passive Poor. High proportions of these groups have a high school education or less, have low incomes (many in poverty), are paid hourly wages in blue-collar occupations or are unemployed. (*See Figure 38.*)

LIFESTYLE

The lifestyle indicator was based on questions about 21 self-reported personal and social activities. Here is a summary:

Enterprisers read more than six books a year for pleasure, exercise frequently and regularly go out to dinner at formal restaurants. They are also more likely than average to attend theater, opera or classical music concerts, work with a youth group, travel overseas and belong to a country club. (Lest you think that Enterprisers are literally "country club Republicans," note that only seven percent of Enterprisers actually do belong to a country club, versus three percent for the population as a whole.) Enterprisers are among the *least* likely to read romance novels or watch nighttime soap operas and religious shows.

Sixties Democrats have a similar lifestyle. All of the activities listed for the Enterprisers also apply to this group, except belonging to a country club. In addition, '60s Democrats enjoy rock 'n' roll along with classical music. They are among the most likely to watch "The Cosby Show" and "Family Ties."

FIGURE 38. SOCIOECONOMIC STATUS

	TOTAL	ENTERPRISERS	MORALISTS	UPBEATS	DISAFFECTEDS	BYSTANDERS	FOLLOWERS	SECULARS	'60s DEMOCRATS	NEW DEALERS	PASSIVE POOR	PARTISAN POOR
Education												
College graduate	18%	41%	13%	20%	9%	5%	9%	43%	40%	7%	7%	7%
Other college	19%	27%	20%	26%	16%	11%	13%	25%	27%	12%	14%	13%
High school graduate	39%	28%	45%	37%	49%	46%	41%	26%	27%	48%	39%	41%
Less than high school graduate	24%	4%	22%	17%	26%	38%	37%	5%	6%	33%	40%	39%
Income												
Less than $10K	16%	2%	13%	11%	15%	26%	21%	9%	6%	16%	30%	30%
$10K-$29,999	45%	31%	46%	46%	48%	47%	53%	36%	40%	40%	46%	51%
$30K-$49,999	24%	35%	26%	28%	24%	20%	15%	30%	35%	25%	12%	12%
$50K +	10%	26%	12%	11%	8%	3%	4%	19%	16%	4%	7%	2%
Occupation												
Professional	30%	59%	32%	33%	20%	16%	16%	56%	46%	16%	19%	15%
Other white collar	7%	5%	8%	10%	8%	6%	10%	7%	7%	6%	6%	9%
Blue collar	38%	16%	31%	40%	44%	59%	46%	21%	32%	36%	43%	51%
Farmer	2%	3%	3%	2%	3%	2%	2%	0%	1%	2%	1%	4%
Nonlabor	18%	13%	21%	11%	19%	11%	20%	15%	11%	34%	27%	15%
Paid												
Salaried	38%	63%	43%	32%	31%	21%	34%	52%	49%	31%	31%	25%
By the hour	46%	19%	41%	54%	53%	59%	47%	38%	37%	49%	50%	59%

Seculars are the third group to enjoy an upper-middle class lifestyle. High proportions of Seculars read six or more books for pleasure, enjoy both classical and rock 'n' roll music, go out to dinner and attend ballet, opera or classical music concerts. They are the most likely group to travel overseas. Seculars have a particular *dislike* of religious shows and nighttime soap operas.

Upbeats watch "Family Ties" and "Cosby," enjoy rock 'n' roll, read more than six books for pleasure, exercise regularly, go camping and participate in sports. A significant proportion also read romance novels.

Disaffecteds enjoy Country and Western music and go camping and hunting in higher proportions than any other group. They are less likely than other groups to watch "Dynasty," "Knots Landing" or "Falcon Crest," or attend the ballet, theater or classical concerts.

Bystanders watch "Family Ties" and "Cosby," watch "Wheel of Fortune" or other game shows, and enjoy Country and Western music, as well as rock 'n' roll. Bystanders are the most likely group to attend discos or other clubs. They do *not* exercise or read for pleasure.

"...'60s Democrats enjoy rock 'n' roll along with classical music."

Followers are least likely to report engaging in any of the activities on the list. Moderately high proportions of Followers watch "Family Ties," "Cosby" and the nighttime soap operas.

Partisan Poor watch "Family Ties" and "Cosby," "Wheel of Fortune" or other game shows and nighttime soap operas. They are heavy viewers of religious shows on television.

Passive Poor have a lifestyle that parallels that of the Partisan Poor.

New Dealers most often report watching game shows and enjoying Country and Western music. They also watch religious shows, and "Dynasty," "Knots Landing" and "Falcon Crest" in higher than average numbers.

Moralists also watch "Family Ties," "Cosby," game shows and nighttime soaps as well as religious shows. However, a significantly *smaller* than average proportion like rock 'n' roll music.

THE TYPOLOGY GROUPS:
BASIC DEMOGRAPHIC DIFFERENCES

11

GENDER

The typology groups are composed of varying proportions of males and females. Most dramatically different are the Enterprisers (60 percent males) and the '60s Democrats (62 percent females). One other group has a significantly higher proportion of males—Disaffecteds (57 percent). Other segments with higher proportions of females include Moralists (55 percent), Upbeats (56 percent), New Dealers (55 percent) and the Partisan Poor (56 percent).

AGE

Upbeats include a larger percentage of younger citizens—42 percent are under 30 years of age. The Bystanders are similar, with 49 percent under 30 years of age. New Dealers (47 percent) and Moralists (33 percent) have a higher proportion of members who are older—60 years plus. Sixties Democrats and Seculars are more likely to be in their thirties or forties.

We finally come to that rapidly aging demographic fad, "yuppies"—those under 40 and college-educated. Despite the best efforts of many to paint them as some type of homogeneous blob interested only in Reeboks, Walkmans and BMWs, "yuppies" are surprisingly diverse. In our typology, "yuppies" are primarily found among several very different segments: '60s Democrats, Seculars, Enterprisers and, to a lesser degree, Upbeats.

RACE AND ETHNICITY

Blacks are distributed across three typology groups in the greatest numbers—Partisan Poor (37 percent), Passive Poor (31 percent) and Followers (25 percent). Hispanics are also found among these groups in the highest proportions, especially Followers. Jews are most likely to be Seculars (11 percent), while Catholics are distributed across all the groups.

"*Despite the best efforts of many to paint them as some type of homogeneous blob interested only in Reeboks, Walkmans and BMWs, 'yuppies' are surprisingly diverse.*"

REGION

Equally high proportions of Followers live in the East (35 percent) and in the South (35 percent). A large percentage of Disaffecteds (32 percent) live in the Midwest. Seculars (16 percent) and '60s Democrats (21 percent) are less likely to live in the South, while Seculars are more often found on the East (31 percent) and West coasts (30 percent). Moralists (39 percent), Partisan Poor (38 percent) and Passive Poor (36 percent) are located in the South in higher proportions than other regions of the country. New Dealers (14 percent) are less likely to live in the West.

UNION HOUSEHOLDS

Union households are distributed across several groups. One in three New Dealers (34 percent) is from a union household. Sixties Democrats, Passive Poor and the Partisan Poor have relatively high proportions of members from union households. Least likely to be a member of a union household are the Enterprisers (9 percent). (*See Figure 39.*)

FIGURE 39. MAJOR DEMOGRAPHICS

	TOTAL	ENTERPRISERS	MORALISTS	UPBEATS	DISAFFECTEDS	BYSTANDERS	FOLLOWERS	SECULARS	'60s DEMOCRATS	NEW DEALERS	PASSIVE POOR	PARTISAN POOR
Sex												
Male	48%	60%	45%	44%	57%	46%	47%	51%	38%	45%	48%	44%
Female	52%	40%	55%	56%	43%	54%	53%	49%	62%	55%	52%	56%
Age												
Under 30	25%	18%	22%	42%	15%	49%	31%	26%	21%	11%	21%	22%
30-39	23%	27%	17%	26%	26%	24%	21%	33%	34%	12%	16%	23%
40-49	16%	20%	13%	13%	23%	11%	13%	15%	21%	11%	15%	21%
50-59	13%	15%	15%	8%	11%	6%	12%	11%	10%	19%	18%	13%
60+	23%	21%	33%	11%	25%	10%	22%	15%	14%	47%	30%	21%
Age by education												
Under 30												
College graduate	3%	7%	1%	6%	*	2%	*	9%	7%	1%	2%	2%
Not college graduate	22%	11%	21%	36%	14%	47%	31%	17%	14%	11%	20%	19%
30-39												
College graduate	7%	14%	4%	8%	4%	1%	3%	17%	17%	2%	2%	3%
Not college graduate	16%	13%	14%	18%	22%	22%	18%	16%	16%	10%	14%	20%
Race & ethnicity												
White	85%	99%	94%	94%	95%	82%	69%	95%	83%	88%	63%	58%
Black	13%	*	5%	4%	4%	13%	25%	3%	16%	11%	31%	37%
Hispanic	7%	3%	5%	5%	3%	12%	18%	3%	3%	4%	10%	11%
Jewish	2%	1%	1%	2%	2%	1%	2%	11%	4%	2%	1%	1%
Catholic	26%	22%	19%	33%	22%	24%	36%	18%	28%	29%	29%	31%
Region												
East	25%	19%	22%	28%	21%	26%	35%	31%	26%	25%	24%	19%
Midwest	24%	25%	20%	27%	32%	23%	14%	23%	28%	27%	24%	25%
South	31%	28%	39%	29%	28%	33%	35%	16%	21%	34%	36%	38%
West	20%	28%	19%	16%	19%	18%	16%	30%	25%	14%	16%	18%
Labor union												
Union household	21%	9%	18%	22%	18%	20%	20%	22%	24%	34%	24%	24%
Non union household	77%	90%	82%	76%	81%	77%	79%	76%	75%	65%	75%	74%

*Less than 0.5 percent.

THE OUTLOOK FOR 1988

12

Almost dead even—that's how the two parties head into the 1988 presidential race.

The Democrats still hold their traditional advantage in party identification. Of the 10 voter typology groups that are politically active, six are aligned with the Democratic Party—translating into a 54 percent to 46 percent Democratic edge in overall affiliation. However, this advantage virtually disappears when the Republicans' higher voter turnout and greater loyalty among their core groups are taken into account. Another apparent Republican advantage that the typology cannot measure is the Electoral College. It gives an edge in presidential contests to the less-populated states, which are often GOP strongholds.

Each party looks at a different road map to victory in 1988. The Republicans must maintain support among independents who lean Republican, while the Democrats must hold onto the party's core groups and minimize defections to the GOP. The Republicans must convert a younger group of voters—the Upbeats—from Ronald Reagan partisans to supporters of the GOP in a post-Reagan era. Second, the Republicans must hold onto another older group that includes many former Democrats—the Disaffecteds—who may return to their roots in the absence of a strong personality like Reagan's.

The Democrats' task is equally daunting, given the defections to Reagan in 1980 and 1984 from all across its party. For example, the policy views of '60s Democrats conflict with Reagan's in most areas, yet one in four (25 percent) of this core Democratic group still voted for the President in 1984. While Republicans continue to have the overall advantage in turnout rates, the old axiom that turnout is only a Democratic problem no longer holds true. The Upbeats, a pro-Republican group, are the youngest cluster and many have yet to become dependable voters. Representing 9 percent of the potential electorate, they are second in importance only to the two core Republican groups for the GOP. The Disaffecteds, another Republican-leaning group, vote at still lower rates, even though their average age is older than the Upbeats.

On balance, there is good news and bad news for both sides. First, the typology provides the following good news for the Republicans:

1. *By stressing American Exceptionalism, Ronald Reagan has attracted the Upbeats to the Republican Party. With the youngest average age of the 11 clusters, the Upbeats are a group that could become a GOP bedrock into the next century.*

2. *Compared to eight years ago, people feel better off about the way things are going in their own lives. In both 1980 and 1984, Reagan capitalized on people's natural tendency to make their voting decisions based on their own pocketbook and the general mood of the country concerning the preceding four years. Issues played less of a role. Our survey finds the public is generally satisfied with their current state of affairs and optimistic about the future. Assuming this continues, it will prompt many to vote Republican.*

3. *Ronald Reagan has broadened the base of the Republican Party beyond its traditional constituencies of the affluent, businessmen and farmers. As other surveys have shown, the typology data reveal strong gains for the GOP among white Southerners. The President's identification with conservative social causes has helped bring significant numbers of white evangelical Christians into the party.*

4. *Ronald Reagan has put together four voter groups as diverse as the old FDR New Deal coalition, laying the base for a potential GOP majority in future elections. The Enterprisers are drawn to the party by economics and the Moralists by social issues, while the Upbeats have responded to Reagan's optimism and the Disaffecteds to his anti-elitist appeal.*

Just as Ronald Reagan is the good news for the Republicans, the President and his administration also created much of the bad news:

1. *As a result of the Iran-Contra affair, the public's positive view of the state of the nation is eroding. This limits the GOP ability to sell the Reagan legacy and to capitalize on people's feelings that they have become personally better off during the Reagan years.*

2. *The Iran-Contra affair has tarnished the Republican image as the party of competent management. This restricts the GOP ability to exploit the Democratic "Jimmy Carter problem" of being seen as poor managers of the federal government.*

3. *Iran-Contra has damaged Republican chances among Disaffecteds, one of the two independent groups that are a key to GOP success. Although Disaffecteds voted for Reagan over Mondale by a four-to-one margin in 1984 and have responded favorably to the President's anti-government themes, many now disapprove of his performance in office. They are highly critical of the Reagan Administration's Central American policy. And the arms sales to Iran were quite damaging to the President's image among a group that expresses very strong animosity toward the Ayatollah's regime.*

4. *While the movement of white evangelical Protestants into the party has added to GOP strength, it has also introduced some division into the Republican ranks. Religion itself divides the solidly Republican ranks more than any other political value. Identification of the party with the social agenda of the Christian right may also hurt the GOP among key swing groups like the Upbeats and Seculars.*

5. *The potential GOP majority depends on four groups that may be very difficult to hold together without a Ronald Reagan at the top of the ticket. Two of the groups are ideological and policy oriented—the Enterprisers and Moralists—while two are non-ideological. The Upbeats respond to themes, while the Disaffecteds respond to personalities. Reagan surely earned his "Great Communicator" fame by conveying four distinct appeals to four distinct groups without turning one against the other. It will be a difficult feat to match.*

"*Religion itself divides the solidly Republican ranks more than any other political value.***"**

Moving to the Democratic side, presidential prospects have certainly brightened since Mondale/Ferraro lost 49 states in 1984. Our typology reveals the following good news for the Democrats:

1. *The Democrats have a strong, unifying value—Social Justice—that seems to strike the right chord with the public today. Opinions about Social Justice relate more strongly than any other political value to candidate preference in our trial heats. This stands in contrast to 1980, when opinions about the parties' abilities to manage the economy were driving the electorate, thus giving a major advantage to the GOP.*

2. *The Democratic Party has substantially improved its image since 1984. This can be explained in part by the GOP's problems with Iran-Contra, plus the fading memory of Jimmy Carter. One key indicator— perceptions of which party is better able to handle the nation's most important problem—now cuts in favor of the Democrats. The party enjoys a strong edge over the GOP among the Seculars and Followers, two key swing groups that lean Democratic, and is roughly even with the GOP among the Disaffecteds, a Republican-leaning group that includes many former Democrats. The public also sees the Democratic Party as better able to bring about the changes the country needs most.*

3. *Each of the four core Democratic groups moved back strongly to their party in the 1986 congressional vote. Disapproval of Reagan is now a unifying theme for them. Particularly heartening for the Democrats is the support given to 1986 Democratic congressional candidates by New Dealers (92 percent), the largest group of Democrats, who gave Ronald Reagan nearly one-third of their vote in 1984.*

4. *Democratic divisions are not being aggravated by foreign policy issues. During Vietnam, differences between hawks and doves shattered the party and helped elect Richard Nixon in 1968. Today, there is no such Democratic division over Central American policy. Both the '60s Democrats and the strongly anti-communist New Dealers and Passive Poor are opposed to the U.S. military involvement in Central America.*

That's the good news. Now, here's the bad news for the Democrats:

1. *The Democrats are still hurt by good times and Americans' optimism about the future. Defections to the Republicans are common among those who feel good about their personal state. This phenomenon is evident among the two more affluent groups—Seculars and '60s Democrats—as well as the New Dealers and the Passive Poor.*

2. *The party continues to have an image problem with regard to competency. Only one-quarter of Seculars (24 percent) and fewer than one-third of '60s Democrats (31 percent) believe the Democrats are better able than the Republicans to manage the federal government.*

3. *The Democrats are divided on spending for the middle class versus spending for the poor. While all the core Democratic groups tend to support increased spending for schools and health care, support levels for programs specifically targeted at blacks and other minorities are sharply lower among New Dealers than among other solidly Democratic blocs. Seculars, the key Democratic-oriented swing group, are also less supportive of social spending for minorities. They prefer to expand benefits for the middle class, such as financial aid for college students.*

4. *The Democrats have an age problem and a persistent loyalty problem. The New Dealers, the largest bloc of Democratic voters, are aging and their influence will wane as memories of FDR and the New Deal continue to fade. The Seculars, a group whose values were formed during the 1960s, agree with the party on most issues, but many in this predominantly baby boom group have failed to become full-fledged Democrats. Finally, the Democratic Party can no longer claim to be the party of youth. The post-baby boom generation has a strong base in the Upbeats, a Republican-oriented cluster.*

Given the pluses and minuses for each party and the lack of an incumbent, the 1988 race promises to be close. The typology data provide us with both a view of how the winning GOP coalition was put together in 1984 as well as detailing what each party must do to win over the key swing constituencies. First, let's look at the makeup of the winning 1984 Reagan coalition.

The Reagan-Bush ticket won a landslide by:

1) *locking up virtually all of the vote among solid GOP clusters;*

2) *pulling in more than three-quarters of the vote among Republican-leaning Upbeats and Disaffecteds;*

3) *splitting the Democratic-oriented Followers vote with Mondale-Ferraro; and*

4) *receiving a sizable proportion of the vote—in some cases more than one-quarter—among other Democratic groups.*

It will be difficult for either party to put together such a sweeping coalition for 1988. Since the primary GOP task is to hold its leaners, while the Democrats must keep their core groups, the battleground will be among the independent and Democratic groups. (Although there are some defections seen in the data among Enterprisers and Moralists, this is probably Iran-Contra fallout, and these staunchly Republican groups will almost certainly return to the fold.)

FIGURE 40. PRESIDENTIAL PREFERENCES (Based on most likely voters)

	1984 national election		1988 trial heat	
	Voted Reagan	Voted Mondale	Favor Bush*	Favor Hart*
Total Republican Groups	92%	7%	69%	23%
Enterprisers	96%	3%	83%	12%
Moralists	98%	2%	79%	12%
Upbeats	86%	13%	51%	41%
Disaffecteds	77%	18%	41%	47%
Total Democratic Groups	26%	70%	17%	77%
'60s Democrats	23%	73%	12%	83%
New Dealers	27%	70%	16%	78%
Passive Poor	26%	72%	22%	72%
Partisan Poor	18%	79%	12%	82%
Seculars	26%	69%	22%	74%
Followers	47%	43%	33%	51%

*Includes leaners.

First, looking at the Republican-leaning groups through the lens of a Bush/Hart trial heat, we find that both groups that voted heavily for Reagan in 1984 will not necessarily vote Republican in 1988. These key swing groups must be wooed by Republicans and Democrats alike. (*See Figure 40.*)

The Upbeats *were attracted to the GOP by Ronald Reagan, and this is one case where evoking the Reagan legacy is not a mixed blessing. They are the only independent group that now approves of Reagan's job performance. The GOP must find a way to move them from being* Reagan *driven to becoming* Republican *driven and reinforce this young group's habit*

of voting Republican. But the GOP must evoke Reagan without alienating other groups for whom the President's luster has faded. The task for the Democrats is to find a way to appeal to this optimistic group in a positive way. "Midnight in America" themes will have the opposite effect.

The Disaffecteds *are attracted to a strong personality who can cut through the bureaucracy, and Ronald Reagan played that role. Since Iran-Contra, however, many have become unhappy with Reagan, and they may tend to return to their largely Democratic roots. The trade issue should play well for the Democrats among the Disaffecteds, who often distrust foreign countries and don't feel they have benefitted from the Reagan economic recovery. This group is a major problem for the Republicans because simply painting the Democrats as the party of big government may not work as effectively as it did in the past.*

Of the two Democratic-leaning independent groups, the *Followers* deserve only brief mention. They vote infrequently and don't have strong

"*The Disaffecteds are attracted to a strong personality who can cut through the bureaucracy, and Ronald Reagan played that role.*"

"*The Seculars could be an electoral sleeping giant.*"

views about issues. The Democrats can appeal to Followers' roots in the party, while the GOP can hope they will follow the crowd toward a popular Republican nominee. The other Democratic-leaning group is considerably more important:

The Seculars *have a poor image of the type of candidates Democrats usually offer and a good image of the times. The GOP can sell it-self as the party that brought about prosperity and is better able to manage the government. However, this group is freedom-oriented, and loss of support among Seculars may be the Achilles' heel of the Republicans as the party expands its appeal among evangelical voters.*

The Seculars could be an electoral sleeping giant. Given their socioeconomic and infor-mation levels, one would expect a high voter turnout, yet voting rates among Seculars are only slightly above average. The Democratic Party's task is to get this group to the polls and get them to vote on the basis of their political beliefs rather than their pocketbooks. The Republicans' chances among Seculars could be helped greatly by a U.S.-Soviet arms agreement, which would effectively neutralize the peace issue.

Moving to the core Democratic groups, the out-look is as follows:

Each party must deal with the '60s Democrats in the same way it deals with Seculars. For the Republicans, this means stressing compe-tency and economic prosperity under Reagan. An arms agreement would certainly improve the GOP's chances among '60s Democrats. Ironically, the Democratic Party is forced to try to impress their own group with the quality of its candidates. Policy positions and turnout are less important concerns—'60s Democrats believe in the Democratic agenda and have very high turnout rates.

New Dealers *and the* Passive Poor *come from different economic levels, but have many similarities with regard to 1988. These Democrats have seen no personal progress under Reagan and have become dissatisfied with the President. There is a sense that Reagan has broken his word that they, too, would share in the good times. These are generally intolerant and hawkish groups, so the Democrats must take care to divert the criticism that the party cares only about blacks, gays and "special interests," but not about the average working person.*

The Partisan Poor *will vote overwhelmingly Democratic. The only question is how energized this voting bloc will be. While there are plenty of signs that opposition to Reagan has increased turnout among this group, the Democrats must preserve their energy until November 8, 1988. On the other hand, the GOP must avoid giving the Partisan Poor incentive to turn out by injecting any racially charged issues into the campaign. In Louisiana, for example, newly elected Democratic Senator John Breaux was helped by the controversy over a GOP plan to challenge voter registration lists in black districts. Republicans cannot afford to let this happen at the national level and risk energizing this group.*

1988
TURNOUT
13

One of the great paradoxes of American democracy is our relatively low level of voter turnout. When asked, three-quarters of the population claim to vote always or nearly always (71 percent). Higher than average proportions of '60s Democrats, Moralists, Enterprisers and New Dealers say they always vote. (*See Figure 41.*)

1988 GENERAL ELECTION TURNOUT

To analyze the 1988 general election about one-half of the total population was classified as likely voters and another one-fifth was classified in a second category—potential voters—based on their past vote and voter registration. (*See Figure 42.*)

FIGURE 41. FREQUENCY OF VOTE

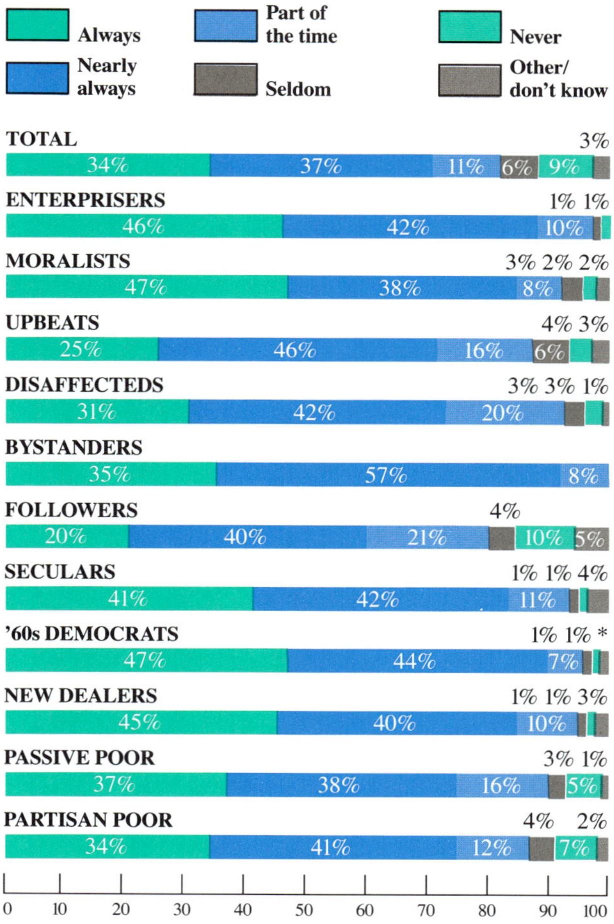

Legend:
- Always
- Nearly always
- Part of the time
- Seldom
- Never
- Other/don't know

Group	Always	Nearly always	Part of the time	Seldom	Never	Other/don't know
TOTAL	34%	37%	11%	6%	9%	3%
ENTERPRISERS	46%	42%	10%		1%	1%
MORALISTS	47%	38%	8%	3%	2%	2%
UPBEATS	25%	46%	16%	6%	4%	3%
DISAFFECTEDS	31%	42%	20%	3%	3%	1%
BYSTANDERS	35%	57%	8%			
FOLLOWERS	20%	40%	21%	4%	10%	5%
SECULARS	41%	42%	11%	1%	1%	4%
'60s DEMOCRATS	47%	44%	7%	1%	1%	*
NEW DEALERS	45%	40%	10%	1%	1%	3%
PASSIVE POOR	37%	38%	16%	5%	3%	1%
PARTISAN POOR	34%	41%	12%	7%	4%	2%

0 10 20 30 40 50 60 70 80 90 100

*Less than 0.5 percent.

FIGURE 42. PROFILE OF 1988 GENERAL ELECTION VOTERS

	Most Likely Voters	Potential Voters	Unlikely Voters	Total
TOTAL	49%	22%	29%	100%

Four voter types are most heavily represented in the likely voters: Enterprisers (16 percent), New Dealers (15 percent), Moralists (14 percent) and '60s Democrats (11 percent). *(See Figure 43.)* By simple numerical advantage, the solid Democratic likely voters outnumber the solid GOP groups by 11 percentage points (41 percent vs. 30 percent). When the proportion of likely voters among the independent groups that lean to each respective party is added to the calculation, the Democratic edge narrows to eight percentage points: Democratic groups, 54 percent vs. Republican groups 46 percent. But the Republican groups may reduce this small advantage because of greater turnout among their partisans. Plus, in recent presidential elections, Republicans have demonstrated greater loyalty in supporting the party's candidates.

A high turnout election has traditionally helped the Democrats, while a low turnout has benefitted the Republicans. But the issue of turnout is no longer that simple. Republicans have broadened their constituency to include younger and less well educated independent groups—Upbeats and Disaffecteds. It will be especially important for the GOP to turn out votes from these groups, as early evidence suggests some decline in defections from the New Dealers to the GOP camp.

The younger than average Upbeats are judged to be the largest group of potential voters in the general election. If the GOP is able to increase their participation in the 1988 election, there would be two positive results: an important group for the future would continue to develop a Republican voting habit, and the numerical

FIGURE 43. DISTRIBUTION OF LIKELY VOTERS IN THE GENERAL ELECTION

	Total	Most likely voters	Potential voters
Solid Republican groups			
Enterprisers	10%	16%	8%
Moralists	11%	14%	10%
	21%	30%	18%
Independent groups leaning Republican			
Upbeats	9%	9%	10%
Disaffecteds	9%	7%	14%
	18%	16%	24%
Independent groups leaning Democratic			
Followers	7%	4%	11%
Seculars	8%	9%	10%
	15%	13%	21%
Solid Democratic groups			
'60s Democrats	8%	11%	9%
New Dealers	11%	15%	11%
Passive Poor	7%	6%	9%
Partisan Poor	9%	9%	8%
	35%	41%	37%
Bystanders (noninvolved)	11%	0%	*

*Less than 0.5 percent.

FIGURE 44. SOUTH VS. NON-SOUTH

| | | Most likely voters | | | | |
| | | South | | | Non-South | |
	Total	**Total South**	**Blacks**	**Whites**	**Blacks**	**Whites**
Solid Republican groups						
Enterprisers	16%	14%	—	18%	*	18%
Moralists	14%	17%	1%	21%	5%	14%
	30%	31%	1%	39%	5%	32%
Independent groups leaning Republican						
Upbeats	9%	9%	3%	10%	4%	10%
Disaffecteds	7%	7%	—	9%	4%	7%
	16%	16%	3%	19%	8%	17%
Independent groups leaning Democratic						
Followers	4%	5%	7%	4%	8%	3%
Seculars	9%	5%	5%	5%	*	11%
	13%	10%	12%	9%	8%	14%
Solid Democratic groups						
'60s Democrats	11%	10%	16%	8%	14%	12%
New Dealers	15%	15%	13%	16%	19%	14%
Passive Poor	6%	7%	19%	4%	17%	4%
Partisan Poor	9%	11%	36%	5%	29%	7%
	41%	43%	84%	33%	79%	37%
Bystanders (noninvolved)	0%	—	—	—	—	—

*Less than 0.5 percent.

advantage of the Democrats in the 1988 general election would be diminished.

Increasing the voter turnout of the Disaffecteds is more problematic. Not only is their devotion to the GOP weak in general, but the Iran-Contra affair has reinforced their alienated, distrustful opinions of government, opinions that are currently directed at Reagan and the Republican Party. Whether they stay at home on election day or shift their support to the Democrats may depend on their final judgment on the Iran-Contra matter, or some other assertive anti-communist activity by the Reagan administration.

Seculars are likely to be an important factor in the 1988 election since they will make up almost one-tenth of the vote. This group is subject to appeals from the GOP as the party that brought good times.

Voter participation among the groups with the largest proportion of blacks and other minorities (Partisan Poor, Passive Poor and Followers) may be influenced by Jesse Jackson's role in the campaign. However, Jackson's efforts to mobilize the minority vote may have a downside in white backlash, particularly in the South.

Since the Republicans already dominate the West, Democrats must pay special attention to the South. In the South, the Democratic groups hold a 6 percentage point advantage (53 percent vs. 47 percent). However, *white* Southerners in the Republican and lean Republican clusters outnumber those in Democratic-oriented clusters by a margin of 16 percentage points (58 percent vs. 42 percent). (*See Figure 44.*)

1988 PRIMARY TURNOUT

The 1988 *Republican Party primaries* will have equal strength between the two major wings of the GOP—the Moralists (33 percent) are about equal in size to the Enterprisers (34 percent). The two independent groups that lean Republican will have much less influence in determining the party's nominee. Even when combined, Upbeats and Disaffecteds (24 percent) make up a smaller share of the likely Republican primary vote than either the Moralists (33 percent) or the Enterprisers (34 percent). However, in the absence of a clear front-runner, or if a large field of Republican contenders splits the vote in the two core GOP wings, Upbeats and Disaffecteds could play a key role in deciding the outcome.

Upbeats and Disaffecteds have very different characteristics. Politically, Upbeats are best grouped with Enterprisers, while Disaffecteds are best grouped with Moralists. Upbeats resemble Enterprisers on American Exceptionalism, in their pro-business sentiments and in their moderation on Militant Anti-Communism; however, unlike Enterprisers, this group favors many

FIGURE 45. REPUBLICAN PARTY PROFILE

	Total population	Total Republicans and leaners	Republican primary likely voters
Enterprisers	10%	27%	34%
Moralists	11%	28%	33%
Upbeats	9%	16%	15%
Disaffecteds	9%	10%	9%
All others	61%	19%	9%
Total	100%	100%	100%

forms of social spending. As a coalition, Enterprisers and Upbeats would make up the largest part of the Republican primary electorate with almost one-half of the likely voters (49 percent). The candidate in the best position to attract Upbeats to the polls would have a base in the Enterpriser group and would have the ability to communicate broad, patriotic themes as opposed to policy-based appeals.

Although Disaffecteds are as large in total numbers in the general population (9 percent) as the Upbeats, their weak affiliation with the Republican Party, combined with their lower propensity to vote, reduces their influence in the primaries to a small fraction. The likely Republican primary vote among Upbeats exceeds that of the Disaffecteds by 6 percentage points. This margin increases dramatically when comparing likely Republican primary voters between Disaffecteds and the solid GOP groups. In fact, with such a high level of alienation, voting participation rates for Disaffecteds may go even lower. This middle-aged, less well educated, predominantly male group has different characteristics from the other Republican groups. Candidates that convey a strong message of assertive anti-communism will appeal to Disaffecteds, as will those who campaign against social spending. Moralists most nearly share these views with Disaffecteds. Taken together, the two groups would make up 42 percent of the likely voters in Republican primaries. (*See Figure 45.*)

FIGURE 46. MOST LIKELY VOTERS IN REPUBLICAN PARTY PRIMARY

	Total	Super Tuesday states		Overall region	
		South	Non-South	South	Non-South
Enterprisers	34%	30%	34%	30%	36%
Moralists	33%	41%	33%	41%	30%
Upbeats	15%	15%	15%	14%	15%
Disaffecteds	9%	7%	13%	8%	10%
All others	9%	7%	5%	7%	9%
Total	100%	100%	100%	100%	100%

FIGURE 47. WHITE EVANGELICAL CHRISTIANS IN GOP PRIMARIES

	Total population	Total Republicans and leaners	Super Tuesday Republican likely primary voters		
			Total	South	Non-South
White evangelical Christians	18%	25%	38%	42%	20%

Moralists (41 percent) will clearly dominate the Republican primaries in the South with a commanding 11 percentage point advantage over the Enterprisers in that region (41 percent vs. 30 percent). In Southern primaries on Super Tuesday, the Moralists' domination over the Enterprisers among likely voters remains equally strong (41 percent vs. 30 percent).

Among likely voters in Republican primaries outside the South, Enterprisers have a 6 percentage point advantage over the Moralists (36 percent vs. 30 percent). However, in the few non-Southern states holding primaries on Super Tuesday, Moralists and Enterprisers will be equally represented among likely primary voters. (*See Figure 46.*)

While white, Protestant evangelicals are only 18 percent of the total population, they make up one-quarter of all Republicans and Republican leaners (25 percent). Most of them are Moralists. However, in Super Tuesday primary states, evangelical Christians make up over one-third (38 percent) of the likely voters in the Republican primary. The proportion of the likely primary voters who are evangelicals in the Southern Super Tuesday states increases to over two in five (42 percent), while outside the South their representation is reduced to one in five (20 percent). (*See Figure 47.*)

This analysis necessarily does not include other factors important to the outcome of the primaries, such as the sequence, uncommitted delegates, caucus states or crossover voting. However, the source of contributions to political candidates and political action groups (PACs) and the relative number of party workers play an important role—not only in determining the strength of partisan commitment, but also in revealing the power of the political types in

FIGURE 48. CAMPAIGN CONTRIBUTORS AND POLITICAL PARTY WORKERS
(Based on most likely voters in Republican party primary)

	Total	Contributed money to		Worked for political party
		Candidates	PACs	
Enterprisers	34%	53%	48%	42%
Moralists	33%	26%	27%	35%
Upbeats	15%	11%	13%	10%
Disaffecteds	9%	5%	7%	6%
All others	9%	5%	5%	7%
Total	100%	100%	100%	100%

determining which candidates will survive the primaries. While less than one in four Republicans very likely to vote in primary elections contributes money to individual candidates, and only 15 percent contribute money to PACs, one-half of these donors come from Enterprisers, and only about one-fourth of the contributions are made by Moralists. So the financial influence of the Enterprisers is nearly double that of the Moralists among probable GOP primary voters. Among those who claim to work for the Republican party, two in five are Enterprisers (42 percent), and one in three is a Moralist (35 percent). *(See Figure 48.)*

Among the Republican candidates measured in the survey, likely Republican primary voters show relatively low levels of familiarity for contenders beyond George Bush, Robert Dole and, to some extent, Alexander Haig. (*See Figure 49.*)

"Likely Republican primary voters show relatively low levels of familiarity for contenders beyond George Bush, Robert Dole and, to some extent, Alexander Haig."

FIGURE 49. NAME RECOGNITION OF REPUBLICAN INTRA-PARTY CANDIDATES

	TOTAL	Likely Republican primary voters			
	TOTAL	ENTERPRISERS	MORALISTS	UPBEATS	DISAFFECTEDS
George Bush	98%	100%	98%	95%	95%
Howard Baker	86%	97%	82%	82%	78%
Robert Dole	85%	97%	83%	78%	70%
Alexander Haig	84%	94%	80%	79%	74%
Pat Robertson	69%	79%	70%	61%	52%
Jack Kemp	64%	78%	62%	47%	48%
Paul Laxalt	43%	60%	37%	29%	22%
Pierre DuPont	37%	52%	28%	33%	20%
Donald Rumsfeld	36%	50%	30%	26%	25%

FIGURE 50. NOMINATION PREFERENCES AMONG REPUBLICAN PARTY CANDIDATES

		Likely Republican primary voters			
	TOTAL	ENTERPRISERS	MORALISTS	UPBEATS	DISAFFECTEDS
George Bush	30%	22%	35%	38%	29%
Howard Baker	18%	23%	12%	18%	17%
Robert Dole	14%	18%	14%	11%	4%
Jack Kemp	8%	12%	6%	4%	3%
Pat Robertson	6%	6%	9%	4%	4%
Alexander Haig	4%	4%	4%	4%	7%
Paul Laxalt	2%	2%	*	3%	2%
Pierre DuPont	1%	1%	1%	2%	—
Donald Rumsfeld	*	1%	—	—	*

*Less than 0.5 percent.

The size of George Bush's lead is at least partially a function of the lack of awareness of other candidates among the typology groups. The preference for Bush is found most strongly among Moralists (35 percent) and Upbeats (38 percent), two groups who are less likely to have heard of Robert Dole, Jack Kemp and the other candidates. (*See Figure 50.*)

Among members of the one typology group most familiar with all the contenders, just over one in five Enterprisers expresses a preference for Bush (22 percent). This relatively weak support for Bush among Enterprisers demonstrates that the nomination is far from being locked up. Robert Dole is able to attract nearly as large a preference from the Enterprisers (18 percent).

Although Pat Robertson's base of support is primarily among evangelical Christians—most often represented in the Moralist cluster—he is not the leader among this group. Bush leads Robertson by 30 percent to 15 percent among white evangelical Christians. (*See Figure 51.*)

The *1988 Democratic primaries* are more complex, with six distinct groups: four solidly

FIGURE 51. PREFERENCES FOR THE REPUBLICAN PARTY NOMINATION
(Based on Republicans and Republican leaners)

	White Protestants	
	Evangelical	Not evangelical
George Bush	30%	37%
Robert Dole	10%	14%
Pat Robertson	15%	2%
Others	26%	29%
None/don't know	19%	18%
	100%	100%

Democratic and two Democratic-oriented independent types. New Dealers are the largest political type among all 11 identified (11 percent of the total population and 22 percent of the Democrats and leaners). This older group has strong roots in the Democratic Party, but has been dissatisfied with the party's recent presidential candidates and platform. Among probable voters in Democratic primaries, New Dealers will be the most dominant single influence, producing nearly one in three votes (27 percent).

The Partisan Poor make up 17 percent of the Democrats and leaners, but are tied with the '60s Democrats as the second most sizable group of likely primary voters (18 percent). Their heavy influence in the Democratic primaries derives from their almost universal affiliation with that party, as well as their high level of voter participation. Candidates that emphasize a strong commitment to social justice will fare best with this group. Three in five of the blacks in this group favor a Jesse Jackson candidacy over other contenders. A strong campaign effort by Jackson could increase this group's voter participation rate in the primaries, especially in the South.

The '60s Democrats are an equally large part of the total population (8 percent) and represent 15 percent of Democrats and leaners. They make up 18 percent of the most likely voters in the primaries.

The Passive Poor are the smallest of the solidly Democratic groups (7 percent), have lower

levels of voter participation and, therefore, will produce the smallest proportion of the most likely primary voters (11 percent).

One of the lean Democratic groups, Seculars may play a key role in the 1988 Democratic primaries. By itself, this group only contributes 12 percent of the probable primary vote. Their relatively small influence in the primary relates to their lower level of affiliation to the party and a lower level of voter participation than their education level would suggest. Their foreign policy preferences and positions on social issues, however, closely resemble those of the '60s Democrats. Together with '60s Democrats, Seculars would have a level of influence equal to that of the New Dealers (30 percent vs. 27 percent).

Followers have a weak attachment to the Democratic Party and very low levels of voter

FIGURE 52. DEMOCRATIC PARTY PROFILE

	Total population	Total Democrats and leaners	Democratic primary likely voters
'60s Democrats	8%	15%	18%
New Dealers	11%	22%	27%
Passive Poor	7%	11%	11%
Partisan Poor	9%	17%	18%
Seculars	8%	12%	12%
Followers	7%	8%	5%
All others	50%	15%	9%
Total	100%	100%	100%

FIGURE 53. MOST LIKELY VOTERS IN DEMOCRATIC PARTY PRIMARY

	Total	Super Tuesday states		Overall region	
		South	Non-South	South	Non-South
'60s Democrats	18%	15%	22%	14%	20%
New Dealers	27%	28%	19%	29%	26%
Passive Poor	11%	14%	6%	13%	9%
Partisan Poor	18%	22%	14%	22%	17%
Seculars	12%	7%	23%	7%	14%
Followers	5%	6%	4%	7%	4%
All others	9%	8%	12%	8%	10%
Total	100%	100%	100%	100%	100%

participation. Only 5 percent of the probable vote in Democratic primaries will be from Followers. (*See Figure 52.*)

In the Southern states on Super Tuesday, New Dealers (28 percent) will outnumber the '60s Democrats (15 percent) and the Seculars (7 percent) by 6 percentage points. This heavy influence of the New Dealers in the Southern Super Tuesday primaries will provide an advantage to candidates perceived as being more moderate on social issues and being in favor of a strong pro-defense agenda. The Partisan Poor will account for one in five (22 percent) votes in Southern Super Tuesday primaries, many of which are likely to be cast for Jackson.

In the few states outside the South that will hold primaries on Super Tuesday, '60s Democrats (22 percent) and Seculars (23 percent) will provide more than two out of every five votes (45 percent). On the other hand, New Dealers will make up about one in five votes (19 percent), and the Partisan Poor will make up one in seven (14 percent) primary votes. (*See Figure 53.*)

A smaller proportion of white evangelical Protestants is found among the Democrat or lean Democrat groups (14 percent) compared to the proportion in the GOP ranks (25 percent). Their presence is most notable among the New Dealers. The proportion of the evangelicals increases to one in five (21 percent) in the Super

"A smaller proportion of white evangelical Protestants are found among the Democrat or lean Democrat groups (14 percent) compared to the proportion in the GOP ranks."

FIGURE 54. WHITE EVANGELICAL CHRISTIANS IN DEMOCRATIC PRIMARIES

	Total population	Total Democrats and leaners	Super Tuesday Democratic likely primary voters		
			Total	South	Non-South
White evangelical Christians	18%	14%	21%	26%	10%

Tuesday states, and they represent one-fourth (25 percent) of the probable electorate in Southern Super Tuesday primaries. Outside the South on Super Tuesday, white evangelical Protestants make up only 10 percent of the likely primary voters. (*See Figure 54.*)

In addition to voter participation rates among the groups, other important influences on the outcome of the Democratic primaries are the financial contributions to candidates and PACs and the number of party workers. Nearly one-third of the contributors among Democratic primary voters will be '60s Democrats. New Dealers are the second largest bloc of money givers, with one-fourth of the contributors to candidates (25 percent) and one-fifth of the donors to PACs (21 percent) coming from this group of likely primary voters. Although Seculars are one of the most upscale groups, their financial contributions are more than 10 percentage points lower than the other upper-middle class group of '60s Democrats. The number of contributors among the Partisan Poor is half that of the '60s Democrats, yet given the financial pressure felt by this group, the proportion of contributors is remarkable. Among those likely to vote in the Democratic Party primary, the '60s Democrats (28 percent) and the New Dealers (23 percent) make up the largest amount of party workers, with the Partisan Poor providing almost equally high proportions (21 percent). Seculars (10 percent) account for less than half the number of party workers among likely voters. (*See Figure 55.*)

FIGURE 55. CAMPAIGN CONTRIBUTORS AND POLITICAL PARTY WORKERS
(Based on most likely voters in Democratic party primary)

	Total	Contributed money to		Worked for party
		Candidates	PACs	
'60s Democrats	18%	30%	32%	28%
New Dealers	27%	25%	21%	23%
Passive Poor	11%	4%	5%	7%
Partisan Poor	18%	14%	12%	21%
Seculars	12%	19%	20%	10%
Followers	5%	3%	3%	4%
All others	9%	5%	7%	7%
Total	100%	100%	100%	100%

The intra-party candidate awareness and preferences show an even more pronounced lack of knowledge about contenders than did the Republicans. Among the candidates other than Jesse Jackson, Gephardt and Dukakis are known more by the Seculars and to a lesser degree by the '60s Democrats, but much less so by the other groups. Because of his high personal awareness, Jesse Jackson is the only candidate to attract a significant number of preferences, with Hart out of the race, among the likely primary voters. (*See Figures 56 and 57.*)

FIGURE 56. NAME RECOGNITION OF DEMOCRATIC INTRA-PARTY CANDIDATES

		Likely Democratic primary voters					
	TOTAL	'60s DEMOCRATS	NEW DEALERS	PASSIVE POOR	PARTISAN POOR	SECULARS	FOLLOWERS
Jesse Jackson	95%	97%	94%	88%	96%	98%	93%
Gary Hart	91%	97%	91%	82%	87%	98%	77%
Bill Bradley	44%	61%	36%	36%	37%	65%	33%
Richard Gephardt	37%	55%	33%	19%	27%	60%	30%
Charles Robb	35%	54%	34%	22%	20%	48%	19%
Sam Nunn	33%	53%	25%	20%	22%	55%	25%
Michael Dukakis	30%	46%	26%	13%	16%	58%	31%
Albert Gore	30%	44%	26%	17%	19%	51%	22%
Bruce Babbitt	25%	41%	20%	17%	15%	43%	16%
Joseph Biden	18%	30%	15%	10%	10%	36%	12%

FIGURE 57. NOMINATION PREFERENCES AMONG DEMOCRATIC PARTY CANDIDATES

		Likely Democratic primary voters					
	TOTAL	'60s DEMOCRATS	NEW DEALERS	PASSIVE POOR	PARTISAN POOR	SECULARS	FOLLOWERS
Jesse Jackson	26%	27%	18%	33%	41%	12%	46%
Bill Bradley	12%	17%	11%	9%	9%	14%	5%
Michael Dukakis	8%	10%	7%	1%	4%	18%	11%
Charles Robb	7%	5%	12%	6%	3%	6%	2%
Richard Gephardt	6%	4%	7%	5%	6%	4%	4%
Sam Nunn	5%	7%	5%	5%	3%	6%	—
Albert Gore	4%	4%	5%	5%	3%	4%	5%
Bruce Babbitt	2%	2%	2%	2%	2%	4%	—
Joseph Biden	2%	4%	1%	2%	1%	2%	—

THE PARTIES

14

In 1987, the two parties are still alive and kicking, but being a Republican or Democrat no longer means all the same things that it did in the past. Our traditional view of the parties—that Republicans are free-enterprise-oriented, affluent and conservative, while Democrats are peace-oriented, social reformers and liberals—holds true for only one-third of the population. For most of the rest, party still matters as a way to help choose candidates, but it has less influence in shaping opinions on issues.

It will shock no one to learn that there is a tendency for Republican-oriented people to rank higher on the socioeconomic scale and to hold views that can frequently be characterized as more conservative than their Democratic counterparts. However, that shorthand analysis has a great many long footnotes weighing it down. Only two Democratic-oriented groups—the Seculars and '60s Democrats—take issues on positions consistently to the left. Two other Democratic groups—the New Dealers and Passive Poor—are just as likely to label themselves conservative as liberal, and their positions on many issues confirm their self-identifications.

While it is true that a Republican group—the Enterprisers—ranks highest in income level and that three Democratic clusters—the Partisan Poor, Passive Poor and Followers—rank lowest in income levels, it is also true that the Seculars and '60s Democrats have income levels that are exceeded only by the solidly Republican Enterprisers.

POLITICAL VALUES

How do the two parties differ? Our survey finds attitudes toward Social Justice—a concept encompassing beliefs about welfarism, egalitarianism and racial equality—to be the single factor that most differentiates those in the solidly Republican clusters from those in the solidly Democratic clusters. Sixty-nine percent of respondents aligned with the Democrats fall on the pro-activist side of the Social Justice scale, while 78 percent of solidly Republican respondents are found at the opposite end of the scale.

Republicans differ somewhat from Democrats on the three factor items measuring basic personal orientations—Religious Faith, Alienation and Financial Pressure. Those in solidly Democratic clusters tend to have stronger religious faith, to have a higher degree of social alienation and to feel more financial pressure than those firmly in the GOP camp. Interestingly, religion may be a source of conflict within the ranks of the Republican Party. There is more variance among the solid GOP clusters on religion than on any other factor item. In fact, such a high level of diversity is not found for any factor among the Democratic groups. This potential conflict between irreligious and religious Republicans is not so much a conflict between Enterprisers and Moralists *per se*. The overall distributions on the Religious Faith scale for these two groups resemble each other quite closely. Rather, there are major differences within the two groups themselves. It is important to keep in mind that the Moralist cluster contains elements of the fundamentalist Protestant movement as well as members of the New Right, for whom religion is not as central to their political beliefs.

Looking at the other five factors that measure political belief, we find the party faithful for the GOP and the Democrats differing least on Tolerance. On the remaining four factors, Republicans are more anti-communist, more suspicious of big government, more pro-business and have a stronger faith in America than Democrats. The largest differences on political values among Democrats are found in their attitudes toward communism.

OPINIONS ON ISSUES

When it comes to issues, the two solidly Republican clusters are more cohesive than the four solidly Democratic clusters. While Republicans tend to be united in their views on a number of social issues and foreign policy/defense issues, Democrats consistently agree on little outside of protectionist legislation, an agenda for federal government social spending and a reluctance to risk U.S. military involvement overseas.

One area where the two solid GOP groups do not concur is on social spending. While the Enterprisers tend to oppose all increases in social spending, Moralists generally favor such spending unless it is specifically targeted to minorities. The groups are also divided on abortion, with the more upscale Enterprisers favoring the status quo on abortion laws, and the

FIGURE 58. GOP OPINION ON ISSUES

	Republican groups	
	Enterprisers	Moralists
Self-described ideology—conservative*	85%	73%
Oppose a tax increase to reduce the federal budget deficit	73%	68%
Favor changing laws to make it more difficult for a woman to get an abortion	40%	60%
Favor a constitutional amendment to permit prayer in public schools	69%	88%
Favor death penalty	78%	85%
Favor "Star Wars"	74%	72%
Oppose cutbacks on defense spending	66%	65%
Unfavorable view of Soviet Union	72%	84%

*Includes leaners.

Moralists, more than any other cluster, favoring new legislation to limit abortions. (*See Figure 58.*)

Not surprisingly, the four solidly Democratic clusters are less often in agreement than the two solid GOP clusters. There is a consensus, however, on protectionist legislation, a key issue in the 1988 campaign for the party's presidential nomination. A second area of consensus among the Democrats is an agenda for federal spending increases. Two-thirds or more of all core Democratic groups favor increased spending in the following areas:
- AIDS research
- Improving health care
- Reducing drug addiction
- Improving the schools
- Programs for the homeless
- Programs for the elderly

On moral and social issues, such as abortion, capital punishment and prayer in schools, there is considerable disagreement among the Democratic rank and file. Sixties Democrats are most consistently tolerant on such issues, while New Dealers are least tolerant. (*See Figure 59.*)

FIGURE 59. DEMOCRATIC OPINION ON ISSUES

	Democratic groups			
	'60s DEMOCRATS	NEW DEALERS	PASSIVE POOR	PARTISAN POOR
Favor increased spending on . . .				
AIDS research	76%	71%	74%	76%
Improving the nation's health care	76%	80%	85%	84%
Programs to reduce drug abuse	68%	77%	75%	74%
Improving the nation's public schools	80%	70%	77%	77%
Programs for the homeless	77%	73%	82%	83%
Programs for the elderly	79%	84%	84%	87%
Social Security	62%	76%	81%	85%
Financial aid to college students	58%	44%	60%	57%
Favor higher taxes on foreign imports to protect American jobs	71%	87%	78%	82%
Changing the laws to make it more difficult for woman to get abortion	26%	54%	47%	38%
Favor death penalty	53%	79%	78%	66%
Favor constitutional amendment to permit prayer in public schools	52%	83%	83%	81%
Feel U.S. military aid to Central America likely to lead to military involvement	86%	76%	66%	75%
Favor cutbacks in defense spending	69%	49%	58%	57%
Oppose developing "Star Wars"	66%	44%	42%	48%

Considering all the differences the solidly Democratic groups have on the issues, there must be other factors keeping people with such diverse views in the party. As previously mentioned, placing a high value on Social Justice is one such factor. All of the core Democratic clusters value Social Justice more than the solid GOP clusters and by majorities of 75 percent and more, identify their party as the one most concerned with the needs and interests of the disadvantaged. The typology data provide strong evidence of another factor that explains the Democratic Party's attraction—a deep-rooted connection to the party and strong parental links. The following table demonstrates this phenomenon. All four core Democratic clusters are more likely than the GOP groups to be connected to the party through parents. And with the exception of the '60s Democrats, the Democratic groups are more likely than the Republican clusters to say they have been a party member "ever since I can remember." (*See Figure 60.*)

PAST VOTE AND FUTURE PREFERENCES

In assessing the parties' strengths and weaknesses, the overall picture is mixed. While it is true that GOP clusters have fewer serious differences among themselves on issues, they have as many differences as Democrats on political values. While Republican groups may have fewer ideological reasons to stray from the party, the Democratic groups are more closely linked to party through family and historical ties. In size, the solidly Democratic groups are larger than the core GOP groups. Independent clusters that lean Republican are not much larger in size than those clusters that lean Democratic.

Despite this lack of evidence that the GOP can easily command majority support among

FIGURE 60. STRENGTH OF PARTY CONNECTION

	Republican groups		Democratic groups			
	ENTERPRISERS	MORALISTS	'60s DEMOCRATS	NEW DEALERS	PASSIVE POOR	PARTISAN POOR
Ever since I can remember I have been a member of the party	49%	64%	59%	86%	72%	82%
My parents were members of the party	46%	49%	63%	81%	68%	75%

the electorate, its success in presidential elections over the past 20 years speaks for itself. Only once in the past 20 years has the Republican ticket lost a presidential election—in 1976, when Carter narrowly defeated Ford. Moreover, the Democrats haven't won an election among whites since LBJ's landslide win over Goldwater in 1964.

In the last two presidential elections, respondents in solidly Republican clusters were more loyal to their party's candidates than were those in core Democratic constituencies. Reagan received over 90 percent of the vote among Enterprisers and Moralists in both 1980 and 1984. Both Carter and Mondale received less than 80 percent of the vote among many of the core Democratic clusters. There is ample evidence, however, that such differences in party loyalty do not hold for all types of elections. The Republican edge in voter loyalty among its core constituencies is less strong at the congressional level, where the Democrats' continued advantage in incumbency obviously is a factor. Many New Dealers and Passive Poor—who voted for Reagan in 1984—did not take the President's advice to back Republicans for Congress in 1986. The largest difference in voting behavior between the two elections is found among the New Dealers, 92 percent of whom supported Democratic congressional candidates in 1986, while only 70 percent supported party nominee Walter Mondale in 1984.

Looking to the future, typology data suggest the Republicans have a potential to repeat their success among three of four core Democratic groups in 1988. Only the Partisan Poor seem more committed to the Democratic Party than they were in 1980. On the other hand, the Republicans may have more trouble in keeping their own troops in line. Currently, solid GOP groups seem no more predisposed to support their party's nominee for president than do their Democratic counterparts. However, this may be an effect of the Iran-Contra affair that will dissipate over time.

Another key to the success of Reagan and the GOP in past elections has been an ability to win an overwhelming share of the vote in the Republican-oriented independent groups and to cut down on or eliminate the Democratic advantage among independents aligned with the opposing party. Upbeats, a group that clearly responds to Reagan's optimism, supported Reagan by 78 percent in 1980 and 86 percent in 1984. He also won a sizable share of the vote among the anti-government Disaffecteds group. Although the Seculars group went Democratic both times, the President still managed a larger share among this group (32 percent) than Mondale captured among the Upbeats (14 percent) and Disaffecteds (17 percent). Among the impressionable Followers, Reagan actually won a greater share of the vote than Mondale in 1984, no doubt capitalizing on his incumbency (54 percent vs. 46 percent).

Looking at the congressional vote in 1986, as well as early presidential preferences for 1988, it appears that the Republicans will have some difficulty repeating Reagan's success among independents. Among the two most politically active independent groups, Seculars are more inclined to vote for a Democrat in 1988 (61 percent) than Upbeats are to support a Republican (47 percent). Moreover, both Bush and Dole failed to win a majority against Hart in the trial heats among Upbeats, while Seculars heavily favored Hart over the two leading Republican contenders. Of course at this stage, before the campaign has captured the public's attention, we can only speculate about general tendencies. If the Republicans nominate a candidate with qualities similar to Reagan's, the GOP could indeed repeat its success among groups like the Upbeats, Disaffecteds and Followers—groups who can be strongly influenced by personal qualities and the ability to communicate themes. At least at this early stage, neither Bush nor Dole has yet to display an appeal as broad as Reagan's, and the other candidates are not yet known to most of the voters.

OUTLOOK FOR THE PARTIES

The typology data do not suggest that the Republicans' success at the presidential level has resulted in a realignment of the electorate or that the Republicans will achieve a majority in the near future. However, there is some evidence of a trend in public sentiment toward the GOP. Since the survey is the first of its kind, we cannot in a strict sense plot a trend over time. But there are other ways to demonstrate such movement to the Republican side.

1. *An analysis of the structure of the typology itself shows that the largest Democratic cluster is the New Dealers, an aging group that is not being replenished by younger segments of the population. The influence of the New Dealers will wane as we move toward the next century. On the other hand, the youngest cluster, the Upbeats, leans Republican. While the Upbeats have not yet moved into the solid GOP ranks, research on voting behavior suggests that party preferences formed in one's youth carry into later stages of life.*

2. *When party orientations are broken out by age groups, we find that the wide advantage*

"There is some evidence of a trend in public sentiment toward the GOP."

enjoyed by the Democrats among older people is greatly reduced among the young. Of those aged 60 and over, 59 percent are in Democratic clusters and 41 percent are in Republican clusters. Those in solidly Democratic clusters outnumber those in solidly GOP groups by almost two to one (47 percent vs. 26 percent). But the Democratic advantage tapers off as age decreases. Among people under 30, the overall Democratic advantage is only 53 percent to 47 percent. But the jury is still out on realignment. Even among the 18-24 group, the Democrats hold a lead among those solidly in party ranks (30 percent vs. 21 percent). Although the proportion in solidly Democratic clusters decreases as age decreases, there is no corresponding increase

FIGURE 61. CLUSTER ORIENTATIONS BY AGE*

	Core Republican groups	Lean Republican groups	Total Republican	Core Democratic groups	Lean Democratic groups	Total Democratic	Democratic advantage
Total	24%	20%	44%	39%	17%	56%	+ 12
Age							
18-24	21%	26%	47%	30%	23%	53%	+ 6
25-29	21%	26%	47%	33%	20%	53%	+ 6
30-39	23%	22%	45%	35%	20%	55%	+ 10
40-49	24%	22%	46%	40%	14%	54%	+ 8
50-59	27%	15%	42%	44%	14%	58%	+ 16
60 +	26%	15%	41%	47%	12%	59%	+ 18

*Bystanders, a group essentially not involved in politics, were excluded from this analysis.

in the size of solidly GOP groups. The size of the independent groups increases instead. It remains to be seen whether the trend will a) continue toward the GOP and produce a realignment; b) stop itself and maintain the Democratic advantage; or, c) produce a dealignment if younger people continue to be independent of either party as they age. (See Figure 61.)

3. Typology analysis shows that 12 percent of the population report having Democratic parents but now fall into Republican-oriented groups. There are fewer cases of the reverse (6 percent), when someone with Republican parents shifts to a Democratic orientation. A breakdown of parent-to-child shifts toward the GOP finds that this shift has occurred disproportionately among white Southerners, white evangelical Protestants and people in business and professional households. In both the South and elsewhere, we find white males more often switching to the GOP than white females. Overall, the shift has been spread evenly among the four Republican-oriented clusters. But what sets the South apart from other regions is the increase in the shift to the Moralist cluster. Another characteristic of the shift in the South is its propensity to come from the New Dealers group.

PARTY CHANGES IN THE SOUTH

Among white Southerners over 50 with some level of political activity, 46 percent have a Republican orientation and 54 percent are Democratic. But among white Southerners under 30, the GOP has an advantage of 61 percent to 39 percent. For whites outside the South, the shift by age is not as extreme. Those over 50 divide 45 percent Republican-oriented vs. 55 percent Democratic; people under 30 divide 51 percent Republican vs. 49 percent Democratic.

A huge gender gap is found in party orientations among Southern whites under 30.

"Issues seem to play an important role in the movement between parties."

Of the males with some political activity, 67 percent are aligned with the GOP, compared with 54 percent of the females. Close to one-third (31 percent) of all white males in the South are classified as Moralists, a group whose numbers are much reduced outside of the South (12 percent).

Issues seem to play an important role in the movement between parties. In fact, the gains that Republicans have made among white Southerners may be partly explained by the issue differences that exist within a specific Democratic group—the New Dealers.

Among the New Dealers, white Southerners and white non-Southerners sharply divide on a number of issues. More specifically, white Southerners are less likely than their non-South New Dealer counterparts to favor increased social spending. Instead, the fiscal conservatism of the white Southern New Dealers closely aligns them with the Republican groups.

In addition, white Southern New Dealers are as reluctant as Republicans to increase spending on programs to assist blacks and other minorities (19 percent vs. 16 percent, respectively). White non-Southern New Dealers, on the other hand, favor increased spending for minority programs at twice those levels (39 percent).

Given the issue differences among the New Dealers, what are the resulting implications? First, the divisions reveal the importance of issues to party politics. Differences between the parties on issues give the GOP an ability to attract significant proportions of white Southerners. More importantly, the defection of white Southerners—a traditionally Democratic constituency—reflects the changing dynamics of the parties. (*See Figure 62.*)

FIGURE 62. ISSUE DIFFERENCES AMONG NEW DEALERS

Favor increased spending on:	Solidly Republican groups	Solidly Democratic groups	New Dealers White South	New Dealers White Non-South
Improving and protecting the environment	48%	65%	46%	62%
Research on AIDS	62%	74%	62%	75%
Programs for the unemployed	21%	55%	34%	51%
Programs that assist blacks/minorities	16%	49%	19%	39%
Programs for the homeless	50%	76%	61%	75%

BLACK
AND
WHITE
POLITICS

15

POLITICAL VALUES

The great divide between black and white Americans is along the line of Social Justice questions: helping the needy and minorities, and ensuring equal opportunity. Close to three in five blacks (58 percent), compared with fewer than one in five whites (17 percent), score high on the Social Justice scale. A second major difference reflects pure economics. Nearly twice as many blacks (41 percent) as whites (22 percent) feel a high degree of financial pressure in their lives.

Two other major differences surface in our survey. About one-half of black Americans (48 percent) score high on Religious Faith; only one-fifth (20 percent) of whites are highly religious. Belief in American Exceptionalism—traditional patriotism in combination with the "can-do" attitude that the country, and U.S. business in particular, can overcome any obstacle—is much stronger among white Americans than among black Americans. Close to one-half of blacks (47 percent) fall into the lowest classification on the American Exceptionalism scale, while only one-fifth of whites (20 percent) have so little faith in America as their black counterparts.

PARTY ORIENTATION

Blacks fall overwhelmingly into solid Democratic or Democratic-oriented groups (79 percent), while whites divide evenly between Democrats (45 percent) and Republicans (44 percent). The majority of blacks (56 percent) are found in three clusters—the Partisan Poor, Passive Poor and Followers—where only 17 percent of whites are found. The Seculars group is the only Democratic-oriented cluster that does not have a sizable black presence. (*See Figure 63.*)

FIGURE 63. DISTRIBUTION OF WHITES AND BLACKS BY CLUSTERS

	Total	Whites	Blacks
Solid Republican groups			
Enterprisers	10%	12%	*
Moralists	11%	12%	4%
	21%	24%	4%
Independent groups leaning Republican			
Upbeats	9%	10%	3%
Disaffecteds	9%	10%	3%
	18%	20%	6%
Independent groups leaning Democratic			
Followers	7%	6%	14%
Seculars	8%	8%	2%
	15%	14%	16%
Solid Democratic groups			
'60s Democrats	8%	8%	11%
New Dealers	11%	12%	10%
Passive Poor	7%	5%	16%
Partisan Poor	9%	6%	26%
	35%	31%	63%
Bystanders (noninvolved)	11%	11%	11%

*Less than 0.5 percent.

POLITICIZATION

One of the major changes in American politics in the 1980s has been the increased participation by poor, less-well-educated blacks. In laying the groundwork for his 1984 campaign, Jesse Jackson played a major role in increasing black voting rates, which now come close to those of whites.

Voter registration rates of *black* Partisan Poor (88 percent) are significantly above those of *white* Partisan Poor (74 percent), and compare favorably to registration among New Dealers and '60s Democrats. Black churches continue to play their traditional role in bringing the Partisan Poor into the political process. Compared with their white counterparts, blacks in the Partisan Poor group score higher on Religious Faith and lower on Alienation.

PARTY LOYALTY

Blacks show greater loyalty to the Democratic Party than whites with similar political beliefs. Blacks are consistently more likely than their white counterparts to say they approve of the Democratic Party's policies and candidates, and are reluctant to vote against a Democratic candidate. Blacks among the Partisan Poor and New Dealers are most loyal to the party, while better-educated black '60s Democrats are more likely to split their tickets.

As blacks move up the socioeconomic scale, they move out of the Partisan Poor, Passive Poor and Followers groups and into the middle-class group of '60s Democrats. No matter how high black Americans climb the socioeconomic ladder, it almost never leads them to the Republican Party. Three-quarters of college-trained blacks (74 percent) are in the core Democratic groups, compared with 59 percent of blacks with no college experience. Close to one-quarter (23 percent) of college-educated blacks are in the Partisan Poor cluster, suggesting that many continue to identify with the concerns of the poor.

The only hopeful sign for the Republicans is that younger blacks may be less overwhelmingly Democratic-oriented than their elders. Close to one in five blacks under 30 (18 percent), compared with half that proportion over 30 (7 percent), is aligned with the GOP. Nearly all of these younger GOP blacks are in the Moralist and Upbeat groups.

FIGURE 64. OPINION ON ISSUES AMONG BLACKS IN FIVE CLUSTERS

	Total Blacks	'60s Democrats	New Dealers	Passive Poor	Partisan Poor	Followers
Favor cutbacks on defense spending	37%	52%	38%	19%	33%	45%
Oppose "Star Wars"	42%	47%	34%	30%	43%	47%
Oppose changing laws to make it more difficult for woman to get abortion	54%	78%	44%	49%	55%	39%
Oppose relaxing environmental controls	36%	50%	30%	33%	33%	32%
Favor death penalty	54%	37%	72%	64%	56%	51%
Favor constitutional amendment to permit prayer in public schools	79%	73%	94%	88%	82%	68%

POLITICAL OPINION

While blacks are solidly Democratic in voting behavior, they are not monolithic in their political values and opinions on issues. Blacks are dispersed through six clusters: five comprising politically active people, and one (the Bystanders) that does not participate in politics at all.

Black '60s Democrats are most consistent in their opinions on issues and in their self-identification. As shown in the following table, they are the black cluster most likely to favor cutbacks in military spending and to oppose anti-abortion legislation and the relaxation of environmental controls. Along with the Followers, they are the group most opposed to "Star Wars."

On the other end of the black Democratic spectrum, black New Dealers make up the cluster that tends to be more moderate on social and moral issues. With the exception of the Followers, they are more likely than other black clusters to favor anti-abortion legislation. Black New Dealers are the black group more inclined to favor the death penalty and prayer in the schools than members of other black clusters.

The black Passive Poor are the cluster scoring highest in terms of being anti-communist and pro-business. This is the most hawkish group on defense issues. They are unwilling to cut defense spending and generally support "Star Wars."

The black Partisan Poor represent the mainstream of black opinion. Their views generally reflect those of all blacks. *(See Figure 64.)*

JESSE JACKSON

Despite the differences in the typology groups, Jesse Jackson's presidential candidacy receives strong support from blacks across the board. *(See Figure 65.)*

FIGURE 65. SUPPORT FOR JESSE JACKSON AMONG BLACKS IN FIVE CLUSTERS

	Choice for Democratic nomination			
	Jesse Jackson	Other candidate	No opinion	Total
Total Blacks	57%	27%	16%	100%
'60s Democrats	56%	31%	13%	100%
New Dealers	56%	30%	14%	100%
Passive Poor	54%	35%	11%	100%
Partisan Poor	60%	27%	13%	100%
Followers	55%	19%	26%	100%

THE
NEW
GENERA-
TION

16

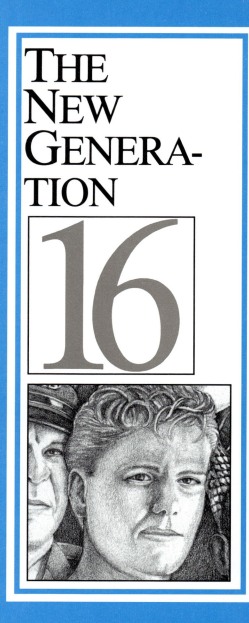

Although the new Times Mirror typology is based on basic beliefs, personal orientations, political involvement and partisan affiliation, several groups emerge with a distinct generational profile. Each of the 11 typology groups is composed of citizens of all age categories; however, on average, New Dealers and Moralists are older; Upbeats and Bystanders are younger; Seculars and '60s Democrats are more middle-aged.

Among four of these groups, the values formed during the time of their political socialization seem more deeply embedded and continue to affect their approach to contemporary politics. This is demonstrated by the combination of beliefs and personal orientations that characterize each group, by their selection of political heroes, by their opinions on issues, and by the nature of their involvement in politics.

As a group, New Dealers were socialized during the period of the Depression, World War II and the McCarthy Era. These Democrats are heavily influenced by the social welfarism of FDR and the strong anti-communist politics of the early 1950s.

Sixties Democrats and Seculars first reached political maturity during the turbulent 1960s. These aging baby boomers, now in their thirties and forties, are influenced by the climate of social change and social equality now symbolized by the Kennedys, Martin Luther King, Jr., and the anti-war and civil rights movements.

Upbeats became politically aware during the Carter years and more importantly during the counterpoint "morning in America" of the Reagan presidency. The age profile of Bystanders closely parallels that of the Upbeats—both groups are heavily composed of members who entered political life during the 1970s and 1980s. However, unlike Upbeats, Bystanders are distinguished by their total lack of involvement in the political process. Thus, while the Democratic Party has an advantage among the older generation and baby boomers, the Republican Party has disproportionately captured the political imagination of the younger generation. (*See Figure 66.*)

FIGURE 66. TYPOLOGY GROUPS BY AGE

	Total	Age		
		Under 30	30-39	40+
Solid Republican groups				
Enterprisers	10%	7%	12%	11%
Moralists	11%	9%	8%	13%
Independent groups leaning Republican				
Upbeats	10%	16%	10%	6%
Disaffecteds	9%	5%	10%	10%
Independent groups leaning Democratic				
Followers	7%	9%	6%	6%
Seculars	8%	8%	11%	6%
Solid Democratic groups				
'60s Democrats	8%	7%	12%	7%
New Dealers	11%	5%	6%	17%
Passive Poor	7%	6%	5%	8%
Partisan Poor	9%	7%	9%	9%
Bystanders (noninvolved)	11%	21%	11%	6%

POLITICAL BELIEFS

Younger and older generations differ significantly in their political beliefs. Americans under 30 years of age are more tolerant, less anti-communist, less religious and more likely to feel financial pressure than older citizens. The young score no differently than the other age groups on Alienation, Social Justice and American Exceptionalism. However, the largest difference found between the generations is that the young are much less likely to hold negative views toward government or big business.

These differences in political beliefs between the younger and older generations show that the young more closely resemble the Republicans on pro-business sentiments and militant anti-communism, but resemble the Democrats on Tolerance and a lack of anti-government sentiments. However, the college-educated under 30, as compared to the less-well-educated young, are significantly more tolerant, hold a more positive view toward Social Justice, are less assertive anti-communists, are more anti-government and hold a somewhat stronger belief in American Exceptionalism.

YUPPIES

There is no separate, single political type that describes the stereotypical "yuppie." Younger, college-educated citizens are found disproportionately among four distinct and very different typology groups.

Seculars, '60s Democrats, Enterprisers and Upbeats are each composed of a significantly large proportion of members under 40 years of age and college-educated. Among the older "yuppies," those in their forties and college-educated, more than two out of five (45 percent) are located in the Republican groups and one-half (53 percent) are found in the Democratic clusters. Younger "yuppies," those in their thirties and college educated, display the same distribution: 44 percent are in the core or leaning GOP groups and 50 percent are solid or leaning Democrats.

Young, white males demonstrate a movement toward the Republicans. Among whites under 30, one in three (34 percent) identifies with the Republican Party, while just over one-fifth (22 percent) affiliate with the Democrats. The differences in partisan affiliation are magnified to a 15 percentage point advantage for the Republicans when independent leaners are included among young whites (51 percent vs. 36 percent).

Young, white women are equally likely to affiliate with either party. The real gender gap is found among the younger generation as compared with the older citizens. Younger, white males are disproportionately Republican (35 percent) compared to younger, white females (26 percent); but older, white males (29 percent) are just as likely to be Republican as older, white females (28 percent). (*See Figure 67.*)

FIGURE 67. PARTY OF WHITES BY AGE AND SEX

	Republicans and leaners	Republicans	Democrats and leaners	Democrats
Total	38%	25%	50%	37%
White males				
Total	45%	30%	43%	30%
Under 30	51%	34%	36%	22%
30-49	46%	27%	43%	27%
50 +	40%	29%	49%	38%
White females				
Total	40%	27%	47%	34%
Under 30	42%	26%	40%	27%
30-49	41%	27%	45%	30%
50 +	38%	28%	55%	42%

political party of the future and the Democratic Party as the party of the past. Two in five white men under 30 years of age selected the Republican Party as forward looking, not old fashioned (40 percent) and as the party that can bring the kind of changes the country needs (40 percent) compared to just over a quarter of the general population. (*See Figure 68.*)

These positive attitudes toward the GOP held by the new generation provide good news for the Republican Party for the future. This is especially important given that one of the largest core Democratic groups, New Dealers, is predominately older. If these findings hold through time, Republicans are positioned to reduce the numerical advantage currently held by the Democrats.

FIGURE 68. VOTING BEHAVIOR AMONG WHITES BY AGE AND SEX

		White males				White females			
	Total	Total	Under 30	30-49	50 +	Total	Under 30	30-49	50 +
1984 vote									
Reagan	40%	48%	36%	51%	53%	44%	28%	48%	48%
Mondale	29%	23%	11%	25%	30%	26%	19%	26%	31%
Other/did not vote	31%	29%	53%	24%	17%	30%	53%	26%	21%
Total	100%	100%	100%	100%	100%	100%	100%	100%	100%
1986 vote									
Republican	40%	47%	50%	50%	44%	42%	40%	44%	40%
Democrat	49%	42%	39%	40%	45%	46%	47%	45%	47%
Other/did not vote	11%	11%	11%	10%	11%	12%	13%	11%	13%
Total	100%	100%	100%	100%	100%	100%	100%	100%	100%

As further evidence of the gender gap among the young, 50 percent of white men under 30 voted Republican in the 1986 congressional election, while only 40 percent of white women under 30 did so. Gender differences among the other age groups are much smaller. Among whites under 30, males voted for Reagan in 1984 by 8 percentage points more than females (36 percent vs. 28 percent), but in the 1986 congressional election, the gap had widened to 10 percentage points (50 percent vs. 40 percent).

Younger, white males are significantly more likely to view the Republican Party as the

TECHNICAL APPENDIX

APPENDIX A—BASIC VALUES AND ORIENTATIONS

Religious Faith

Religious Faith is an overall measure of belief in God. It measures the degree to which the public feels religion is an important part of life. The key items comprising this factor reflect a belief in fundamental religious doctrine—consciousness of God, literal interpretation of the Bible, etc.—as well as the importance of prayer.

Key Variables Associated with Religious Faith

A higher religious orientation is found among two key demographic groups—females and blacks. Nearly half of the females (47 percent), compared with one-third (32 percent) of the males, are deeply religious. Slightly more than six in 10 (61 percent) blacks score high. In addition, those who reside in the South are more likely to be religious than people living elsewhere (49 percent vs. 36 percent). College graduates (32 percent) and those under 30 years of age (32 percent) have lower than average numbers with a strong religious belief.

In terms of political characteristics, there are no significant differences by party affiliation. But citizens who are fairly active in political affairs are more likely to be highly religious than the general population. More than four in 10 (44 percent) likely voters, compared to only one-third (33 percent) of those not likely to vote, report being highly religious. Moreover, equally high proportions of both Democrats (45 per-

cent) and Republicans (44 percent) who report that they are very likely to vote also have a strong religious orientation.

Tolerance/Intolerance

Tolerance/Intolerance gauges the extent to which citizens value civil liberties, freedom of expression, free choice and acceptance of others who choose a different lifestyle. Included are issues that have been debated throughout American history—freedom of speech, the banning of books, the right to censor news stories and the rights of criminal suspects. In addition, Tolerance/Intolerance encompasses feelings about traditionalism—the role of women in society and values toward marriage, the family and child rearing.

Key Variables Associated with Tolerance/Intolerance

The less educated and older segments of the population tend to be the most intolerant. More than six in 10 of those with an incomplete high school education (62 percent) and those 60 years of age and older (61 percent) are intolerant, as are over one-half (53 percent) of those aged 50-59.

The college educated and those under age 40 are less likely to be intolerant (19 percent and 33 percent respectively). In addition, significantly smaller proportions (26 percent) of upper-income households ($40,000 and over) are intolerant.

Non-participants in political affairs tend to score high on Intolerance. More than one-half of those who have not voted in the last two national elections (53 percent), and 48 percent of those not registered to vote are intolerant.

Social Justice
Social Justice measures the strength of beliefs about welfarism, equality, consciousness of social class standing and the role of government in providing for the needy. This factor also embraces attitudes toward the position of blacks, the role of labor unions and the division between rich and poor.

Key Variables Associated with Social Justice
Nearly four-fifths (78 percent) of blacks, compared with one-third of whites (31 percent), score high on this item. In addition, less educated and low-income individuals hold stronger positive feelings about social justice; one-half of those with less than a high school education (51 percent) and an equal proportion (50 percent) of people who live in households earning less than $10,000 income score high. Strong beliefs about Social Justice are concentrated in the East. Nearly one-half of Easterners (45 percent) scored high on this factor, while one-third (36 percent) of respondents in other regions felt strongly about Social Justice.

As might be expected, larger proportions of Democrats (55 percent) scored high on the Social Justice factor than did Republicans (21 percent). More than one-half (56 percent) of those "very likely" to vote in the Democratic primary have strong beliefs about Social Justice.

Militant Anti-Communism
Militant Anti-Communism has three interrelated components: perceptions about the threat of communism, feelings about militarism and the use of force to further American interests, and ethnocentrism—the belief that America, as well as its citizens, is superior to others.

Key Variables Associated with Militant Anti-Communism
Militant Anti-Communism is found in higher than average proportions among both less-educated and older segments of the population. One-half (53 percent) of those who did not graduate from high school and an almost equally large proportion of high school graduates (47 percent) score high on this factor.

Other demographic groups having strong anti-communist beliefs include those:
- *Aged 50 and older (51 percent)*
- *Earning less than $10,000 in annual household income (50 percent)*
- *Residing in the South (49 percent)*

People who score high on this factor are just as likely to call themselves Democrats as Republicans.

Alienation
Alienation represents the degree to which people hold feelings of powerlessness, hopelessness, personal cynicism and a distrust of the political system. Several of the items explore the concept of Alienation in personal terms by examining the perceived control the individual has over his/her own life and the extent to which the individual feels at the mercy of outside forces. More generally, this factor measures feelings about the relationship of the individual to the political system.

Key Variables Associated with Alienation
Of the total population, 42 percent score high on the Alienation factor. As one might suspect, there are two demographic groups that tend to be alienated in higher proportions than average: the less educated and those with lower income.

In terms of party affiliation, Republicans (31 percent) are less likely to score high on alienation. While Democrats are not a particularly alienated group, higher than average proportions of those who disapprove of Reagan (48 percent) score high on alienation.

On the Likely Voter Index, nearly six in 10 (57 percent) of those "not likely" to vote are alienated. High proportions of the following groups are also more alienated than average Americans:
- *Those who have not voted in the last two national elections (62 percent)*
- *Those who are not registered (58 percent)*
- *Those who scored low on the knowledge of public affairs scale (52 percent)*

Attitudes toward Government
Attitudes toward Government measures beliefs about the size, power and effectiveness of government. It marks feelings about federal government intrusion into personal life and

beliefs about grass-roots politics, as well as more general perceptions about the desirability of regulation and control.

Key Variables Associated With Attitudes toward Government

Negative attitudes toward government prevail among older segments of the population. Over one-half of those aged 60 and above (52 percent), compared with 40 percent of the total population, hold anti-government attitudes. Those living in the West and the Midwest are also more likely to hold strong negative feelings about government. On the other side of the coin, certain demographic groups have a low degree of anti-government feelings, including:

- *The young, aged 18-24 (22 percent vs. 40 percent of total population)*
- *Blacks (30 percent vs. 40 percent)*
- *Hispanics (30 percent vs. 40 percent)*

Republicans are more likely than Democrats (46 percent vs. 37 percent) to hold negative attitudes toward government. Reagan supporters tend to score high on anti-government sentiments.

Interestingly, active participants in political affairs also score high on anti-government feelings. Opposition to a big and powerful system of government is not a major mark of the uninvolved nor the disillusioned segments of the population. Instead, those interested in politics are the ones who are most critical of the waste and inefficiency in government.

American Exceptionalism

American Exceptionalism represents a belief in America that combines traditional patriotism with a view that our country has an infinite capacity to solve its problems. A third element in this factor is the feeling that American vitality is due to the success of American business.

Key Variables Associated with American Exceptionalism

American Exceptionalism can be found across nearly all demographic groups. Only when analyzing race do significant differences among groups emerge. Nearly one-half of whites (46 percent) say they are patriotic, but among blacks, less than one-quarter (23 percent) volunteer this response.

Republicans are more likely than Democrats to hold views summarized as American Exceptionalism (51 percent vs. 38 percent). Reagan's supporters are a critical element in this factor.

Financial Pressure

Financial pressure measures the degree of financial concern felt by the respondents. While this factor is determined significantly by income itself, it goes beyond an objective measure of dollars and cents to reflect the *perception* of one's financial status.

Key Variables Associated with Financial Pressure

Not surprisingly, the poorest demographic groups—blacks, hispanics, the less educated—score high on this factor. Six in 10 (60 percent) blacks and more than one-half of the hispanics (53 percent) express concern. Smaller proportions of those earning $40,000 or more (19 percent) and those who have a college education (22 percent) score high on financial concern.

Those who do not participate in the political process appear most likely to be burdened with financial cares. More than one-half (54 percent) of those not registered to vote, compared with only one-third (35 percent) of those registered, score high on Financial Pressure.

Attitudes toward Business Corporations

Attitudes toward Business Corporations represents a belief about the size, power and role of American business. This factor associates specifically with "big business"—the concentration of power and the fairness of business practices (especially with regard to the level of profits).

Key Variables Associated with Attitudes toward Business Corporations

Among the total sample, four in 10 (41 percent) hold anti-business sentiments. The only group that hold such beliefs in proportions higher than average is labor union households (50 percent). And while no other groups are strongly anti-business, several groups appear to support big business. Compared with the total sample (41 percent), significantly smaller proportions of blacks (34 percent), people under age 30 (34 percent) and people earning $50,000 a year or more (33 percent), have a negative attitude toward business.

Party identification and other political variables also help define the elements of the

FIGURE 69. SELF-IDENTIFICATION*

Items	Does not identify 1-5	Identify 6+	Strongly identify 8+
Religious person	28%	71%	49%
Feminist/supporter of the women's movement**	46%	51%	29%
Environmentalist	31%	66%	39%
Republican	65%	31%	20%
Democrat	52%	44%	31%
Liberal	59%	34%	19%
Conservative	49%	45%	27%
National Rifle Association supporter	55%	39%	27%
Union supporter	54%	43%	27%
Supporter of business interests	44%	52%	28%
Anti-communist	20%	78%	70%
Pro-Israel	46%	43%	25%
Supporter of the peace movement	40%	65%	46%
Supporter of the civil rights movement	29%	68%	47%
Supporter of the anti-abortion movement	52%	44%	32%
Supporter of the gay rights movement	79%	18%	8%

*Respondents were asked to self-identify with 16 items on a scale of 1-10 where "1" is a description that is totally wrong for them and "10" is a description that is perfect.

**Females were asked to self-identify with the term "feminist," while males were asked to self-identify with "a supporter of the women's movement."

business factor. Democrats are more likely than Republicans to oppose big business (46 percent vs. 35 percent). Knowledge of public affairs is also correlated with sentiments about business: nearly one-half (45 percent) of those scoring high on the knowledge scale are critical of big business.

APPENDIX B—MEASURING SELF-IDENTIFICATION

In addition to looking at how basic predispositions relate to public opinion, we also examined how Americans self-identify themselves politically. People were asked the extent to which they self-identify with 16 terms. (*See Figure 69.*)

The terms that Americans identify with most strongly (8+ on the 1-10 scale) are anti-communist (70 percent), a supporter of the civil rights movement (47 percent), a supporter of the peace movement (46 percent) and an environmentalist (39 percent). The least popular self-identification is a supporter of the gay rights movement, with only 8 percent strongly identifying.

As an identity, anti-communism is virtually universal in America. Those segments of the population that regard themselves as anti-communist in higher than average proportions include:

- *Aged 50+ (78 percent)*
- *Republicans (80 percent)*
- *Approve of Reagan (78 percent)*
- *Voted for Reagan twice in national elections (82 percent)*

Forty-seven percent strongly identify with the civil rights movement. Not surprisingly, 84 percent of blacks regard themselves as civil rights supporters.

Significant proportions of those who regard themselves as supporters of peace are Democrats (54 percent) and disapprove of Reagan (53 percent).

Those who strongly identify with an environmentalist are found in higher than average proportions among males (44 percent) and the college educated (50 percent). Environmentalists are less likely than the national average to be black (31 percent) and to be under 30 years of age (34 percent). Significant proportions of environmentalists are also likely to vote (45 percent) and score high on the knowledge scale (47 percent).

Those who identify with the women's movement in higher than average numbers are found in the following two groups:

- *Black (39 percent)*
- *College-educated (34 percent)*

Surprisingly, there are no differences in identification by sex; females are *no* more likely than males to identify with the women's movement (30 percent vs. 27 percent).

Identification with unions and with business is nearly equal. Similar proportions strongly identify with each (27 percent and 28 percent, respectively). But on balance, support for business outweighs support for unions. When identification is more broadly defined as a score of six or higher, 52 percent identify with business interests, compared with 43 percent identifying with unions.

In turning to special-interest groups, there are significant proportions, but not majorities, identifying with pro-Israel, the anti-abortion movement and the National Rifle Association. Even though these special-interest groups don't attract majorities, their levels are comparable to or greater than those found for the political labels. Four in 10 expressed some identification with NRA (39 percent), pro-Israel (43 percent) and anti-abortion (44 percent), while 31 percent identify with Republican and slightly higher proportions identify with liberal (34 percent), Democrat (44 percent) and conservative (45 percent). Anti-abortion supporters are disproportionately Catholic (39 percent) and less educated (39 percent). Conversely, smaller proportions of anti-abortion supporters reside in the West (26 percent) or earn $50,000 or more in annual income (21 percent) and few score high on the knowledge scale (26 percent).

Those identifying with anti-abortion show no significant differences in party affiliation or past vote, yet more than one-third (37 percent) say they are conservative and approve of Reagan (34 percent).

Slightly more than one-quarter (27 percent) of the total sample *strongly* identify with National Rifle Association supporter. In particular, significant proportions of NRA supporters are male (36 percent). Among the population groups who are *less* likely than the national sample to identify with NRA supporter are the following:

- *Blacks (15 percent)*
- *College-educated (16 percent)*
- *Easterners (23 percent)*

The key demographic characteristic of those identifying with pro-Israel is religion. It's no surprise that 86 percent of Jews regard themselves as pro-Israel. The politically involved and knowledgeable also tend to be pro-Israel identifiers.

Only 8 percent strongly identify with the term supporter of the gay rights movement. Among those most likely to regard themselves as supporters of gay rights are:

- *College-educated (14 percent)*
- *Jewish (29 percent)*

Identification with political labels is relatively weak. One-fifth of Americans *strongly* identify with Republican (20 percent) or liberal (19 percent), while only slightly greater proportions identify with conservative (27 percent) and Democrat (31 percent). Some GOP faithful will be disheartened to note that among the 16 identifications, Republican is third only to liberal and gay rights as items *least* identified with among Americans.

Democrats have a decided numerical edge over Republicans, yet conservatives are more populous than liberals. So there is an unusually large bloc of Americans who self-identify as both Democrat and conservative.

Other measures of partisanship and ideology confirm these findings. The standard party affiliation question reveals that the proportion of Democrats is larger than that of Republicans (37 percent vs. 25 percent), yet on the ideology measure, conservatives outnumber liberals (43 percent vs. 30 percent). The highest proportions of respondents are found among those who are either: (1) Democrat and liberal (24 percent) or (2) Republican and conservative (26 percent). However, an almost equally large proportion of respondents say they are both Democrat and conservative (18 percent). The loneliest group are those who claim to be Republican and liberal (8 percent).

Further Observations on Self-Identification

- *Anti-communism is not as prevalent among younger segments of the population. People under 40 years of age are less likely than those older to strongly identify with anti-communist (61 percent vs. 76 percent).*
- *In several cases, the level of education among the young results in differences in identification. The educated young (under 30 years of age) are less likely than their counterparts with fewer years of schooling to regard themselves as anti-abortion supporters (14 percent vs. 31 percent) or National Rifle Association supporters (20 percent vs. 30 percent).*
- *Men and women differ in their levels of identification on several items. The most significant difference is found on support for the National Rifle Association. Males are more likely than females to strongly identify with NRA (36 percent vs. 18 percent). Also,*

males tend to identify with environmentalist in greater proportions than females (44 percent vs. 35 percent). Conversely, females are more likely than males to strongly identify with religion (56 percent vs. 41 percent) and with the peace movement (50 percent vs. 43 percent). Interestingly, females are no more likely than males (30 percent vs. 27 percent) to support the women's movement.

- *The political issue identifications—peace, civil rights, environment, women's movement and gay rights—are all highly correlated. In particular, support for civil rights is a strong indicator of support for peace (and vice versa).*

APPENDIX C—SUMMARY OF SURVEY METHODOLOGY

For the purpose of this research project, personal and telephone interviews were conducted among adult Americans on two separate occasions.

The Pilot Telephone Survey

Between January 28-February 1, 1987, Gallup interviewed a national sample of 508 adults by telephone. This pilot study tested the proposed questionnaire for the principal survey. It also provided a preview of what the eventual typology analysis might show.

The Principal Personal Interview Survey

Face-to-face personal interviews were conducted among a nationally representative sample of 4,244 adults. Interviews were conducted during the period April 25-May 10, 1987. The margin of error due to sampling is ± 2 percentage points. The sampling procedures used included a special oversample of black adults.

THE DESIGN OF THE PERSONAL INTERVIEW SAMPLE

The sampling procedure is designed to produce an approximation of the adult civilian population, 18 years and older, living in the United States, except those persons in institutions such as prisons or hospitals.

The design of the sample is that of a replicated, probability sample down to the block

level in the case of urban areas, and to segments of townships in the case of rural areas. Over 300 sampling locations were used in each survey.

The sample design includes stratification by these seven size-of-community strata, using 1980 Census data: (a) incorporated cities of population 1,000,000 and over; (b) incorporated cities of population 250,000 to 999,999; (c) incorporated cities of population 50,000 to 249,999; (d) urbanized places not included in (a)-(c); (e) cities of population 2,500 or over outside of urbanized areas; (f) towns and villages with less than 2,500 population; and (g) rural places not included within town boundaries. Each of these strata are further stratified into four geographic regions: East, Midwest, South and West. Within each city size-regional stratum, the population is arrayed in geographic order and zoned into equal sized groups of sampling units. Pairs of localities are selected in each zone, with probability of selection and each locality proportional to its population size in the 1980 census, producing two replicated samples of localities.

Separately for each survey, within each subdivision so selected for which block statistics are available, a sample of blocks or block clusters is drawn with probability of selection proportional to the number of dwelling units. In all other subdivisions or areas, blocks or segments are drawn at random or with equal probability.

In each cluster of blocks and each segment so selected, a randomly selected starting point is designated on the interviewer's map of the area. Starting at this point, interviewers are required to follow a given direction in the selection of households until their assignment is completed.

Interviewing is conducted at times when adults, in general, are most likely to be at home, which means on weekends, or if on weekdays, after 4:00 P.M. for women and after 6:00 P.M. for men. Interviewers made multiple trips to the selected interviewing areas. On each trip after the first they were instructed to call back at households where no one was available for an interview on prior visits. On average, interviewers made three trips to each area in an effort to complete the assignment and obtain the participation of hard-to-reach respondents.

Although "call-backs" were made for this survey, an additional allowance for persons not at home is made by a "times-at-home" weighting procedure. This procedure is a standard method for reducing the sample bias that would otherwise result from underrepresentation in the sample of persons who are difficult to find at home.

The pre-stratification by regions is routinely supplemented by fitting each obtained sample to the latest available Census Bureau estimates of the regional distribution of the population. In addition, minor adjustments of the sample are made by educational attainment by men and women separately, based on the annual estimates of the Census Bureau (derived from their Current Population Survey) and by age and race.

COMPOSITION OF THE SAMPLE FOR THE PRINCIPAL SURVEY

	Weighted Percentage	Number of Interviews
Sex		
Male	47.9	(2,123)
Female	52.1	(2,121)
	100.0	(4,244)
Race		
White	84.8	(3,397)
Black	12.6	(755)
Other	2.3	(77)
Undesignated	0.3	(15)
	100.0	(4,244)
Age		
18-29 years	25.3	(867)
30-49 years	38.9	(1,658)
50 years and older	35.5	(1,707)
Undesignated	0.3	(12)
	100.0	(4,244)
Education		
College graduate	18.0	(859)
Other college	18.4	(812)
High school graduate	39.3	(1,634)
Less than high school graduate	24.0	(930)
Undesignated	0.3	(9)
	100.0	(4,244)

COMPOSITION OF THE SAMPLE FOR THE PRINCIPAL SURVEY

	Weighted Percentage	Number of Interviews
Region		
East: Maine, New Hampshire, Rhode Island, New York, Connecticut, Vermont, Massachusetts, New Jersey, Pennsylvania, West Virginia, Delaware, Maryland, District of Columbia	30.0	(1,337)
Midwest: Ohio, Indiana, Illinois, Michigan, Minnesota, Wisconsin, Iowa, North Dakota, South Dakota, Kansas, Nebraska, Missouri	23.3	(1,019)
South: Kentucky, Tennessee, Virginia, North Carolina, South Carolina, Georgia, Florida, Alabama, Mississippi, Texas, Arkansas, Oklahoma, Louisiana	27.6	(1,121)
West: Arizona, New Mexico, Colorado, Nevada, Montana, Idaho, Wyoming, Utah, California, Washington, Oregon, Alaska, Hawaii	19.1	(767)
	100.0	(4,244)

SURVEY QUESTIONNAIRE

100. Do you approve or disapprove of the way Ronald Reagan is handling his job as President?
47% Approve
44% Disapprove
<u>9%</u> Don't know
100%

101. Thinking ahead to the 1988 Presidential election, are you in *general* more likely to vote for a Republican candidate for President or for a Democratic candidate for President?
30% Republican
40% Democratic
2% Other
20% IT DEPENDS *(VOLUNTEERED)*
<u>8%</u> Don't know
100%

102. What does it mean to you when someone says he or she is a *Republican*? *(PROBE)*

Conservative	21%
Money/power	18%
Business oriented	13%
Agrees with GOP platform	8%
Unconcerned with needs of the people	5%
Other	40%
Don't know	14%

103. What does it mean to you when someone says he or she is a *Democrat*? *(PROBE)*

For working people/people oriented	21%
Liberal	18%
Person who votes Democratic	9%
Spends too much money	7%
Cares for poor/disadvantaged	7%
Other	39%
Don't know	13%

104.* Generally speaking, would you say that *you personally* care a good deal which party wins the presidential election in 1988 or that you don't care very much who wins?
54% Care a good deal
40% Don't care very much
<u>6%</u> Don't know
100%

104.* Generally speaking, would you say that *you personally* care a good deal who wins the presidential election in 1988 or that you don't care very much which party wins?
76% Care a good deal
20% Don't care very much
<u>4%</u> Don't know
100%

105. *(HAND RESPONDENT Card A)* Will you please look over this list of Republicans and tell me which of them you have *heard of.* Please read off your answers by number. *(INTERVIEWER: CIRCLE NUMBERS. RESPONDENT RETAINS Card A THROUGH Q. 107.) (See Card A)*
1 2 3 4 5 6 7 8 9 0 None/DK
(SKIP TO Q. 108)

106. Next, which ONE would you like to see nominated as the Republican Party's candidate for president in 1988? Please read off your answer by number. *(INTERVIEWER: CIRCLE ONE NUMBER ONLY.)*
1 2 3 4 5 6 7 8 9 0 None/DK
(SKIP TO Q. 108)

107. And who would be your SECOND choice? Please read off your answer by number. *(INTERVIEWER: CIRCLE ONE NUMBER ONLY.)*
1 2 3 4 5 6 7 8 9 0 None/DK

*Each question was only asked of half the sample.

BASED ON REPUBLICANS AND REPUBLICAN LEANERS
(Q's. 105-107) Card A

	HEARD OF	1ST CHOICE	1ST AND 2ND CHOICE
1. Howard Baker	82%	16%	33%
2. George Bush	97%	33%	49%
3. Robert Dole	81%	13%	41%
4. Pierre Du Pont	32%	1%	2%
5. Alexander Haig	78%	5%	14%
6. Jack Kemp	59%	7%	13%
7. Paul Laxalt	37%	1%	3%
8. Pat Robertson	62%	5%	9%
9. Donald Rumsfeld	32%	*%	1%
None/don't know	1%	18%	27%
Did not respond to list		1%	1%
		100%	

BASED ON DEMOCRATS AND DEMOCRATIC LEANERS
(Q's. 108-110) Card B

	HEARD OF	1ST CHOICE	CANDIDATE PREFERRED WITH HART OUT OF RACE
1. Bruce Babbitt	22%	1%	2%
2. Joseph Biden	16%	1%	2%
3. Bill Bradley	43%	7%	12%
4. Michael Dukakis	27%	5%	8%
5. Richard Gephardt	33%	2%	5%
6. Albert Gore	26%	2%	4%
7. Gary Hart	87%	38%	—%
8. Jesse Jackson	92%	18%	26%
9. Sam Nunn	28%	3%	5%
10. Charles Robb	30%	3%	6%
None/don't know	3%	17%	30%
Did not respond to list		3%	N/A%
		100%	

ASK EVERYONE:

108. *(HAND RESPONDENT Card B)* Will you please look over this list of Democrats and tell me which of them you have *heard of*. Please read off your answers by number. *(INTERVIEWER: CIRCLE NUMBERS. RESPONDENT RETAINS Card B THROUGH Q. 110.) (See Card B)*

01　02　03　04　05　06　07　08　09　10

109. Next, which ONE would you like to see nominated as the Democratic Party's candidate for president in 1988? Please read off your answer by number. *(INTERVIEWER: CIRCLE ONE NUMBER ONLY.)*

01　02　03　04　05　06　07　08　09　10
　　　　　　　　　　　　　　　　　　00　None/DK
　　　　　　　　　　　　　　　　(SKIP TO Q. 111)

110. And who would be your SECOND choice? Please read off your answer by number. *(INTERVIEWER: CIRCLE ONE NUMBER ONLY.)*

01　02　03　04　05　06　07　08　09　10
　　　　　　　　　　　　　　　　　　00　None/DK

ASK EVERYONE:

111. Suppose the 1988 presidential election were being held TODAY. If George Bush were the Republican candidate and Gary Hart were the Democratic candidate, which would you like to see win?

　38% Bush
　47% Hart
　　3% Other
　12% Undecided
100%

112. As of today, do you lean more to Bush, the Republican, or to Hart, the Democrat?

Bush and leaders　　　40%
Hart and leaners　　　49%

ASK EVERYONE:

113. If Robert Dole were the Republican candidate and Gary Hart were the Democratic candidate, which would you like to see win?

　33% Dole
　50% Hart
　　2% Other
　15% Undecided
100%

114. As of today, do you lean more to Dole, the Republican, or to Hart, the Democrat?

Dole and leaners　　　34%
Hart and leaners　　　52%

ASK EVERYONE:

115. If Robert Dole were the Republican candidate and Ted Kennedy were the Democratic candidate, which would you like to see win?

　39% Dole
　49% Kennedy
　　2% Other
　10% Undecided
100%

116. As of today, do you lean more to Dole, the Republican, or to Kennedy, the Democrat?

Dole and leaners　　　39%
Kennedy and leaners　　51%

ASK EVERYONE:

117. What do you think is the most important problem facing this country today?

Unemployment/recession/depression	13%
Federal budget deficit	12%
Threat of nuclear war	7%
Economy	7%
Poverty/hunger	6%
Drug abuse	6%
Arms race	4%
Foreign affairs	3%
Crime	3%
Trade deficit	3%
Moral decline	3%
Other	31%
Don't know	2%

118. Which political party do you think can do a better job of handling the problem you have just mentioned—the Republican Party or the Democratic Party?

28% Republican
38% Democratic
24% No difference *(VOLUNTEERED)*
10% Don't know
100%

Now on a more personal subject…

119. All of us want certain things out of life. When you think about what really matters in your own life, what are your wishes and hopes for the future. In other words, if you imagine your future in the *best* possible light, what would your life look like then if you are to be happy? Take your time in answering; such things are not easy to put into words.

Personal economic situation	26%
Good health	22%
Job/work situation	21%
Own wishes and hopes	20%
War/peace	19%
Family life	15%
Other	61%
Don't know	2%

120. Taking the other side of the picture, what are your fears and worries of the future? In other words, if you imagine your future in the *worst* possible light, what would your life look like then? Again, take your time in answering.

Poor health	20%
Fear of nuclear war	17%
Lack of financial security	17%
Fear of war (general)	16%
Unemployment	16%
Recession/depression/inflation	11%
Loss of family	7%
Other	52%
Don't know	3%

(See Card C for Questions 121-126)

121. *(HAND RESPONDENT Card C)* Here is a ladder representing the "ladder of life." Let's suppose the top of the ladder represents the *best* possible life for you; and the bottom, the *worst* possible life for you. On which step of the ladder do you feel you personally stand at the present time? *(INTERVIEWER: CIRCLE ONE NUMBER. RESPONDENT RETAINS Card C THROUGH Q. 126.)*

DK
00 01 02 03 04 05 06 07 08 09 10 99

122. On which step would you say you stood *five years ago*? *(INTERVIEWER: CIRCLE ONE NUMBER.)*

DK
00 01 02 03 04 05 06 07 08 09 10 99

RESPONDENT'S LADDER OF LIFE (MEAN VALUES)
(Q's. 121-123) Card C

FIVE YEARS AGO	TODAY	FIVE YEARS FROM NOW		
5.8%	6.5%	7.7%	10	Best Possible
			9	
			8	
			7	
			6	
			5	
			4	
			3	
			2	
			1	
			0	Worst Possible

U.S. LADDER OF LIFE (MEAN VALUES)
(Q's. 124-126) Card C

FIVE YEARS AGO	TODAY	FIVE YEARS FROM NOW		
5.7%	5.5%	6.1%	10	Best Possible
			9	
			8	
			7	
			6	
			5	
			4	
			3	
			2	
			1	
			0	Worst Possible

123. Just as your best guess, on which step do you think you will stand in the future, say about *five years from now*? *(INTERVIEWER: CIRCLE ONE NUMBER.)*

DK
00 01 02 03 04 05 06 07 08 09 10 99

124. Looking at the ladder again, suppose the top represents the *best* possible situation for our country; the bottom, the *worst* possible situation. Please tell me on which step of the ladder you think the United States is at the present time. *(INTERVIEWER: CIRCLE ONE NUMBER.)*

DK
00 01 02 03 04 05 06 07 08 09 10 99

125. On which step would you say the U.S. was about *five years ago*? *(INTERVIEWER: CIRCLE ONE NUMBER.)*

DK
00 01 02 03 04 05 06 07 08 09 10 99

126. Just as your best guess, if things go pretty much as you now expect, where do you think the U.S. will be on the ladder, let us say, about *five years from now*? *(INTERVIEWER: CIRCLE ONE NUMBER.)*

DK
00 01 02 03 04 05 06 07 08 09 10 99

127. Compared to five years ago, would you say you are *better off* financially, *worse off* financially or *about the same*?

48% Better off
20% Worse off
31% About the same
  1% Don't know
100%

128. Compared to five years ago, would you say the U.S. is *more* respected by other countries, *less* respected by other countries or *as* respected as it was five years ago by other countries?

19% More
55% Less
23% As respected
  3% Don't know
100%

129. Compared to five years ago, would you say our military defenses are *stronger, weaker* or about the *same*?

41% Stronger
16% Weaker
37% About the same
  6% Don't know
100%

130. Compared to five years ago, would you say there is a *greater* chance of a nuclear war, a *lesser* chance of a nuclear war or about the *same* chance?

32% Greater
20% Less
44% About the same
  4% Don't know
100%

131. Do you happen to know, is the U.S. supporting those who oppose the government in Nicaragua or is the U.S. supporting the Nicaraguan government against the rebels?

45% U.S. supporting the opposition
16% U.S. supporting the government
39% Not sure/Don't know
100%

132. Compared to five years ago, has the federal budget deficit increased, decreased or stayed about the same?

74% Increased
 9% Decreased
 8% Stayed about the same
 9% Don't know
100%

133. *(HAND RESPONDENT Card D)* Do you happen to know which of these men is *currently* the White House Chief of Staff—Who?

 7% James Baker
 8% Alexander Haig
49% Howard Baker
13% Donald Regan
 * Other answer
23% Don't know
100%

NO QUESTIONS 134-199

*Less than 0.5 percent.

200. If you had a say in making up the federal budget this year, for which of the following programs would you like to see spending increased, for which would you like to see spending decreased or for which should spending be kept the same? First... *(INTERVIEWER: READ LIST. CIRCLE ONE NUMBER FOR EACH ITEM.)*

		INCREASED	SAME	DECREASED	DON'T KNOW	
a.	Improving and protecting the environment?	59%	34%	4%	3%	= 100%
b.	Financial aid for college students?	43%	41%	13%	3%	= 100%
c.	Social Security?	64%	31%	3%	2%	= 100%
d.	Research on AIDS?	69%	21%	7%	3%	= 100%
e.	Aid to the Contras in Nicaragua?	9%	22%	56%	13%	= 100%
f.	Government assistance for the unemployed?	41%	41%	15%	3%	= 100%
g.	Scientific research?	45%	42%	9%	4%	= 100%
h.	Programs that assist blacks and other minorities?	35%	44%	18%	3%	= 100%
i.	Improving the nation's health care?	72%	23%	3%	2%	= 100%
j.	Reducing drug addiction?	66%	24%	8%	2%	= 100%
k.	Improving the nation's public school system?	69%	25%	4%	2%	= 100%
l.	Military armaments and defense?	24%	44%	29%	3%	= 100%
m.	Programs for the homeless?	67%	25%	5%	3%	= 100%
n.	Aid to farmers?	58%	28%	10%	4%	= 100%
o.	Programs for the elderly?	75%	21%	2%	2%	= 100%

201. *(HAND RESPONDENT Card E)* The following is a list of some programs and proposals that are being discussed in this country today. For each one, please tell me whether you strongly favor, favor, oppose or strongly oppose. The first one is... *(INTERVIEWER: READ LIST. CIRCLE ONE NUMBER FOR EACH ITEM.)*

		STRONGLY FAVOR	FAVOR	OPPOSE	STRONGLY OPPOSE	DON'T KNOW	
a.	Changing the laws to make it more difficult for a woman to get an abortion	18%	23%	33%	18%		
			41%		51%	8%	= 100%
b.	A mandatory death penalty for anyone convicted of premeditated murder	35%	37%	18%	5%		
			72%		23%	5%	= 100%
c.	A constitutional amendment to permit prayer in the public schools	30%	41%	17%	8%		
			71%		25%	4%	= 100%
d.	The "Star Wars" program to develop a space-based defense against nuclear attack	13%	39%	25%	11%		
			52%		36%	12%	= 100%
e.	Cutting back federal spending for defense and military purposes	13%	35%	38%	8%		
			48%		46%	6%	= 100%
f.	Mandatory drug tests for government employees	24%	41%	22%	8%		
			65%		30%	6%	= 100%
g.	Relaxing environmental controls in order to allow more economic growth and development	7%	31%	34%	19%		
			38%		53%	9%	= 100%
h.	Proposals to limit the access that AIDS patients have to public places	11%	29%	39%	10%		
			40%		49%	11%	= 100%
i.	Proposals to increase the federal income tax to reduce the federal deficit	4%	24%	44%	21%		
			28%		65%	7%	= 100%
j.	Proposals to increase taxes on foreign imports to protect American jobs in certain industries	28%	47%	16%	4%		
			75%		20%	5%	= 100%
k.	Resuming the military draft	10%	33%	39%	12%		
			43%		51%	6%	= 100%

202. *(HAND RESPONDENT Card F)* Notice that the 10 boxes on this card go from the highest position of +5 for a country you have a very favorable opinion of all the way down to the lowest position of -5 for a country you have a very unfavorable opinion of. How far up the scale or how far down the scale would you rate... *(READ LIST. CIRCLE ONE NUMBER FOR EACH ITEM.)*

		VERY UNFAVORABLE	UNFAVORABLE	FAVORABLE	VERY FAVORABLE	DON'T KNOW	
		-5 -4	-3 -2 -1	+1 +2 +3	+4 +5	00	
a.	Iran	58%	28%	6%	1%	7%	= 100%
b.	Canada	*	3%	37%	57%	3%	= 100%
c.	Soviet Union	33%	38%	23%	2%	4%	= 100%
d.	Japan	7%	20%	55%	14%	4%	= 100%
e.	Israel	6%	21%	47%	18%	8%	= 100%
f.	Great Britain	1%	5%	50%	38%	6%	= 100%
g.	China	5%	23%	57%	8%	7%	= 100%
h.	South Africa	27%	36%	24%	5%	8%	= 100%
i.	West Germany	3%	13%	56%	19%	9%	= 100%
j.	Mexico	4%	23%	56%	11%	6%	= 100%

*Less than 0.5 percent.

203. *(HAND RESPONDENT Card G)* Now let's compare the U.S. to Japan, Great Britain, West Germany and other major western countries in the world on a number of factors. Would you say today that the United States is very strong, strong, weak or very weak compared to other countries in the following areas... *(READ ITEMS. CIRCLE ONE NUMBER FOR EACH ITEM.)*

		U.S. VERY STRONG	U.S. STRONG	U.S. WEAK	U.S. VERY WEAK	DON'T KNOW	
a.	Our system of public education	10%	38%	40%	7%	5%	= 100%
b.	Production of quality products	9%	47%	37%	4%	3%	= 100%
c.	Technical innovation	19%	51%	21%	2%	7%	= 100%
d.	Overall standard of living	35%	51%	10%	1%	3%	= 100%

204. Should the U.S. be giving assistance to the Contras, that is, the guerilla forces now opposing the Marxist government in Nicaragua?

26% Yes
56% No
18% Don't know
100%

205. Do you feel the U.S. military aid to Central America is likely to lead to U.S. military involvement in that area?

68% Yes
19% No
13% Don't know
100%

206. Which do you think is the greater cause of unrest in Central America today: subversion from Cuba, Nicaragua and the Soviet Union *or* poverty and lack of human rights in the area?

19% Subversion from Cuba, Nicaragua and the Soviet Union
51% Poverty and lack of human rights
18% BOTH EQUALLY *(VOLUNTEERED)*
12% Don't know
100%

207. Some people feel the U.S. should try to develop a space-based "Star Wars" system to protect the U.S. from nuclear attack. Others oppose such an effort because they say it would be too costly and further escalate the arms race. Which position comes closer to your view?

44% Should develop a space-based "Star Wars" system
42% Oppose developing such a system
14% Don't know
100%

208. At the present time, which nation do you feel is stronger in terms of military power, the United States or the Soviet Union—or do you think they are about equal militarily?
    23% U.S.
    25% Soviet Union
    46% About equal
     6% Don't know/no opinion
    100%

209. To reduce tensions with the Soviet Union, do you think U.S. policy is too willing to compromise, not willing enough to compromise or about right?
    22% Too willing
    23% Not willing enough
    46% About right
     9% Don't know
    100%

210. In your opinion, which of the following increases the chances of nuclear war more—a continuation of the nuclear arms build-up here and in the Soviet Union OR the U.S. falling behind the Soviet Union in nuclear weaponry?
    42% Nuclear arms build-up
    41% U.S. falling behind
    17% Don't know
    100%

211. Should the U.S. use military force against terrorist organizations or nations that harbor terrorists even if there is a risk that civilians may be killed?
    61% Yes
    27% No
    12% Don't know
    100%

212. In your opinion, which is the greater risk to peace—trusting the Russians to live up to their side of an arms agreement or being too suspicious of the Russians so that we never get an arms agreement with them?
    43% Trusting Russians
    41% Being too suspicious
    16% Can't say/Don't know
    100%

NO QUESTIONS 213-299

Now on a completely different subject...

300. In politics, as of today, do you consider yourself a *Republican*, a *Democrat*, an *Independent* or what?
    25% Republican
    37% Democrat
    28% Independent
     8% No preference
      * Other party
     2% Don't know
    100%

IF "REPUBLICAN" IN Q. 300, ASK Q. 301
301. Would you call yourself a *strong* Republican or a *not very strong* Republican? *(Based on Republicans—25%)*
    11% Strong
    14% Not strong
    25%

*Less than 0.5 percent.

302. Tell me if any of these statements come close to what you mean when you say you are a Republican. *(INTERVIEWER: READ LIST. CIRCLE ONE NUMBER FOR EACH ITEM.) (Based on Republicans)*

		YES	NO	DON'T KNOW	
a.	I usually think of myself as a Republican but I don't agree completely with what the party stands for	78%	18%	4%	= 100%
b.	I usually prefer Republican candidates but sometimes I support Democrats	77%	21%	2%	= 100%
c.	I involve myself in what the Republican Party is doing	32%	64%	4%	= 100%
d.	I'm a Republican but it isn't very important to me	37%	59%	4%	= 100%
e.	I'm a Republican because of the way I feel about what Ronald Reagan has been doing	32%	66%	2%	= 100%
f.	With me it's more a matter of not liking the Democrats than anything else	18%	78%	4%	= 100%

IF "DEMOCRAT" IN Q. 300, ASK Q. 303.

303. Would you call yourself a *strong* Democrat or a *not very strong* Democrat? *(Based on Democrats—37%)*

18% Strong
<u>19%</u> Not strong
37%

304. Tell me if any of these statements come close to what you mean when you say you are a Democrat. *(INTERVIEWER: READ LIST. CIRCLE ONE NUMBER FOR EACH ITEM.) (Based on Democrats)*

		YES	NO	DON'T KNOW	
a.	I usually think of myself as a Democrat but I don't agree completely with what the party stands for	70%	25%	5%	= 100%
b.	I usually prefer Democratic candidates but sometimes I support Republicans	66%	32%	2%	= 100%
c.	I involve myself in what the Democratic Party is doing	36%	61%	3%	= 100%
d.	I'm a Democrat but it isn't very important to me	37%	60%	3%	= 100%
e.	With me it's more a matter of not liking the Republicans than anything else	20%	74%	6%	= 100%

IF "INDEPENDENT" OR "NO PREFERENCE" OR "OTHER" IN Q. 300, ASK Q. 305. OTHERS GO TO Q. 306.

305. Would you say you lean more to the Republican Party or more to the Democratic Party? *(Based on Independents, Other, No Preference)*

13% Republican
13% Democratic
<u>12%</u> Don't know
38%

ASK EVERYONE:

306. *(HAND RESPONDENT Card H)* As I read each of the following statements, tell me if, for you, it applies more to the Democratic Party, more to the Republican Party or to neither party. The first one is… *(INTERVIEWER: READ LIST. CIRCLE ONE NUMBER FOR EACH ITEM.)*

		REPUBLICAN PARTY	DEMOCRATIC PARTY	NEITHER PARTY	DON'T KNOW	
a.	Ever since I can remember I have been a member of this party	20%	41%	36%	3%	= 100%
b.	My parents were members of this party	24%	48%	18%	10%	= 100%
c.	I'm involved in this party in my own community	9%	17%	70%	4%	= 100%
d.	I generally like the policies of this party	32%	43%	20%	5%	= 100%
e.	I like the kinds of candidates run by this party	31%	37%	25%	7%	= 100%
f.	I find it hard to vote against the candidates of this party	19%	28%	45%	8%	= 100%

307. When it comes to politics, do you usually think of yourself as a liberal, a conservative or what?

30% Liberal
43% Conservative
3% Other *(VOLUNTEERED)*
15% Neither
<u>9%</u> Don't know
100%

LIBERAL AND LEANERS	CONSERVATIVE AND LEANERS
35	48

308. Do you think of yourself as a *strong* liberal or *not very strong* liberal? *(Based on Liberals)*
    10% Strong
    20% Not very strong
    ___*___ Don't know
    30%

309. Do you think of yourself as a *strong* conservative or a *not very strong* conservative? *(Based on Conservatives)*
    17% Strong
    25% Not very strong ⎫ GO TO Q. 313
    ___1%___ Don't know ⎭
    43%

310. Do you think of yourself as more *like* a liberal or more *like* a conservative? *(Based on those who say they are other, neither, don't know)*
    4% Liberal
    5% Conservative
    9% Neither *(VOLUNTEERED)*
    ___8%___ Don't know
    26%

ASK EVERYONE:
311. What does it mean to you when someone says they are a *liberal*? *(PROBE)*

Acceptable to change/flexible	17%
Support programs that increase spending	17%
Someone open-minded	13%
Favors social programs	9%
Believe in rights of all people	8%
Other	37%
Don't know	18%

312. What does it mean to you when someone says they are a *conservative*? *(PROBE)*

Resistant to change	21%
Thrifty	17%
Traditional/old-fashioned	8%
Reasonable/practical	8%
Narrow-minded/prejudiced	6%
Middle-of-the-road	5%
Other	38%
Don't know	15%

ASK EVERYONE:
313. Thinking of the Democratic and Republican Parties, would you say there is a great deal of difference in what they stand for, a fair amount of difference or hardly any difference at all?
    25% A great deal
    45% A fair amount
    25% Hardly at all
    ___5%___ No opinion/Don't know
    100%

314. *(HAND RESPONDENT Card I)* Now I'm going to read you a few phrases. For each, I'd like you to tell me whether you think that the phrase better describes the *Republican Party* or the *Democratic Party*. How about the phrase... *(READ FIRST ITEM)?* Does that more accurately describe the Republican Party and its leaders or the Democratic Party and its leaders? *(READ LIST. CIRCLE ONE NUMBER FOR EACH ITEM.)*

		DESCRIBES REPUBLICAN	DESCRIBES DEMOCRATIC	(VOL) BOTH	(VOL) NEITHER	DK/NO OPINION	
a.	Is well organized	34%	19%	25%	13%	9%	= 100%
b.	Selects good candidates for office	27%	26%	25%	13%	9%	= 100%
c.	Is concerned with the needs and interests of the disadvantaged	11%	61%	14%	7%	7%	= 100%
d.	Is forward-looking, not old-fashioned	27%	38%	16%	9%	10%	= 100%
e.	Has a common-sense approach to problems	28%	35%	15%	14%	8%	= 100%
f.	Is able to manage the federal government well	24%	25%	13%	28%	10%	= 100%
g.	Can bring about the kinds of changes the country needs	26%	36%	14%	14%	10%	= 100%
h.	Is concerned with the needs and interests of business and other powerful groups	58%	15%	16%	3%	8%	= 100%

*Less than 0.5 percent.

315. *(HAND RESPONDENT Card J)* Now I'd like to ask you a question about how you regard yourself. On a scale from 1 to 10, where "10" represents a description that is perfect for you and "1" a description that is totally wrong for you, how well do each of the following describe you? First, to what extent do you *regard* yourself as… *(READ LIST. CIRCLE ONE NUMBER FOR EACH ITEM.)*

		DESCRIPTION TOTALLY WRONG 1	2	3	4	5	6	7	8	DESCRIPTION PERFECT 9	10	DON'T KNOW	
a.	A religious person	4%	3%	4%	4%	13%	9%	13%	20%	11%	18%	1%	= 100%
b.	A feminist (for women)												
b.	A supporter of the women's movement (for men)	10%	6%	6%	6%	18%	11%	11%	14%	7%	8%	3%	= 100%
c.	An environmentalist	2%	2%	5%	6%	16%	12%	15%	15%	10%	14%	3%	= 100%
d.	A Republican	34%	7%	7%	4%	13%	6%	6%	7%	4%	8%	4%	= 100%
e.	A Democrat	21%	6%	6%	6%	13%	6%	7%	9%	6%	16%	4%	= 100%
f.	A liberal	21%	7%	9%	7%	15%	8%	7%	8%	4%	7%	7%	= 100%
g.	A conservative	15%	6%	7%	7%	14%	9%	9%	11%	7%	9%	6%	= 100%
h.	A union supporter	18%	7%	7%	8%	14%	8%	9%	8%	5%	13%	3%	= 100%
i.	A supporter of business interests	7%	4%	6%	8%	19%	11%	12%	14%	7%	8%	4%	= 100%
j.	An anti-communist	8%	2%	2%	2%	6%	3%	5%	8%	10%	52%	2%	= 100%
k.	Pro-Israel	12%	4%	6%	6%	18%	10%	8%	10%	5%	10%	11%	= 100%
l.	A National Rifle Association supporter	24%	7%	6%	6%	11%	6%	6%	8%	5%	14%	7%	= 100%
m.	A supporter of the peace movement	6%	3%	4%	5%	12%	9%	10%	13%	10%	23%	5%	= 100%
n.	A supporter of the civil rights movement	6%	2%	4%	4%	13%	9%	12%	15%	10%	22%	3%	= 100%
o.	A supporter of the anti-abortion movement	23%	6%	6%	6%	11%	6%	6%	7%	7%	18%	4%	= 100%
p.	A supporter of the Gay Rights movement	50%	9%	7%	5%	10%	4%	3%	3%	2%	4%	3%	= 100%

NO QUESTIONS 316–399

400. *(HAND RESPONDENT Card K)* Now I am going to read you a series of statements that will help us understand how you feel about a number of things. For each statement, please tell me whether you *completely* agree with it, *mostly* agree with it, mostly *disagree* with it or *completely* disagree with it. The first one is… *(INTERVIEWER: CIRCLE ONE NUMBER FOR EACH ITEM.)*

		COMPLETELY AGREE	MOSTLY AGREE	MOSTLY DISAGREE	COMPLETELY DISAGREE	DON'T KNOW	
a.	People like me don't have any say about what the government does	14%	38%	34%	12%	2%	= 100%
b.	Generally speaking, elected officials in Washington lose touch with the people pretty quickly	22%	51%	21%	3%	3%	= 100%
c.	Most elected officials care what people like me think	5%	42%	40%	9%	4%	= 100%
d.	Voting gives people like me some say about how the government runs things	23%	55%	15%	4%	3%	= 100%
e.	Success in life is pretty much determined by forces outside our control	8%	30%	41%	16%	5%	= 100%
f.	Hard work offers little guarantee of success	7%	22%	44%	24%	3%	= 100%
g.	The federal government should be able to overrule individual states on important matters	8%	36%	33%	14%	9%	= 100%
h.	The strength of this country today is mostly based on the success of American business	16%	60%	16%	3%	5%	= 100%
i.	Government regulation of business usually does more harm than good	12%	43%	30%	4%	11%	= 100%
j.	When something is run by the government, it is usually inefficient and wasteful	19%	44%	27%	4%	6%	= 100%
k.	The federal government should run *only* those things that cannot be run at the local level	22%	53%	16%	3%	6%	= 100%
l.	The federal government controls too much of our daily lives	18%	40%	32%	5%	5%	= 100%
m.	The government is really run for the benefit of all the people	9%	48%	31%	8%	4%	= 100%

		COMPLETELY AGREE	MOSTLY AGREE	MOSTLY DISAGREE	COMPLETELY DISAGREE	DON'T KNOW	
n.	Business corporations generally strike a fair balance between making profits and serving the public interest	4%	39%	38%	10%	9%	= 100%
o.	There is too much power concentrated in the hands of a few big companies	27%	50%	16%	2%	5%	= 100%
p.	Business corporations make too much profit	21%	44%	24%	4%	7%	= 100%
q.	It is time for Washington politicians to step aside and make room for new leaders	16%	46%	26%	3%	9%	= 100%
r.	Dealing with a federal government agency is often not worth the trouble	14%	44%	29%	3%	10%	= 100%
s.	As Americans we can always find a way to solve our problems and get what we want	12%	56%	24%	4%	4%	= 100%
t.	I don't believe that there are any real limits to growth in this country today	17%	50%	24%	4%	5%	= 100%
u.	We need new people in Washington even if they are not as effective as experienced politicians	9%	35%	38%	10%	8%	= 100%
v.	Our society should do what is necessary to make sure that everyone has an equal *opportunity* to succeed	37%	53%	7%	1%	2%	= 100%
w.	We have gone too far in pushing equal rights in this country	11%	31%	37%	16%	5%	= 100%
x.	It is the responsibility of the government to take care of people who can't take care of themselves	21%	50%	20%	4%	5%	= 100%
y.	The government should help more needy people even if it means going deeper in debt	13%	40%	33%	7%	7%	= 100%
z.	The government should guarantee every citizen enough to eat and a place to sleep	22%	40%	26%	7%	5%	= 100%
aa.	I like political leaders who are willing to make compromises in order to get the job done	16%	56%	16%	4%	8%	= 100%
bb.	I don't pay attention to whether a candidate calls himself a liberal or a conservative	14%	47%	26%	7%	6%	= 100%
cc.	I am very patriotic	43%	46%	7%	1%	3%	= 100%
dd.	In the past few years there hasn't been much real improvement in the position of black people in this country	8%	28%	45%	14%	5%	= 100%
ee.	I think it's all right for blacks and whites to date each other	13%	35%	22%	24%	6%	= 100%
ff.	We should make every possible effort to improve the position of blacks and other minorities, even if it means giving them preferential treatment	6%	18%	43%	28%	5%	= 100%
gg.	Discriminations against blacks are rare today	6%	28%	43%	18%	5%	= 100%
hh.	It is my belief that we should get even with any country that tries to take advantage of the United States	11%	33%	37%	10%	9%	= 100%
ii.	The best way to ensure peace is through military strength	14%	40%	30%	10%	6%	= 100%
jj.	American lives are worth more than the lives of people in other countries	7%	17%	39%	32%	5%	= 100%
kk.	We all should be willing to fight for our country, whether it is right or wrong	17%	37%	27%	13%	6%	= 100%
ll.	I often worry about the chances of a nuclear war	23%	39%	27%	0%	2%	= 100%
mm.	Most of the countries that have gotten help from America end up resenting us	21%	50%	19%	2%	8%	= 100%
nn.	It's best for the future of our country to be active in world affairs	32%	55%	7%	1%	5%	= 100%
oo.	There is an international communist conspiracy to rule the world	22%	38%	21%	7%	12%	= 100%
pp.	Communist and non-communist countries can learn to live together peacefully	18%	50%	18%	6%	8%	= 100%
qq.	Communist countries are all alike	9%	28%	40%	11%	12%	= 100%
rr.	Communists are responsible for a lot of the unrest in the United States today	17%	39%	27%	8%	9%	= 100%

401. *(HAND RESPONDENT Card L)* Now, I'd like your opinion on some people. As I read from a list, please tell me which category on this card best describes your *overall* opinion of the person I name. Probably, there will be some names on this list that you have never heard of. First, how would you describe your opinion of... *(READ ITEM)? (INTERVIEWER: CIRCLE ONE NUMBER FOR EACH ITEM.)*

		VERY FAVORABLE	MOSTLY FAVORABLE	MOSTLY UNFAVORABLE	VERY UNFAVORABLE	NEVER HEARD OF	DON'T KNOW	
a.	Billy Graham	22%	44%	16%	10%	2%	6%	= 100%
b.	Dan Rather	24%	60%	6%	2%	3%	5%	= 100%
c.	Geraldine Ferraro	6%	42%	26%	12%	4%	10%	= 100%
d.	Robert Dole	9%	51%	11%	3%	9%	17%	= 100%
e.	Barbara Walters	16%	58%	14%	5%	2%	5%	= 100%
f.	Richard Nixon	7%	32%	34%	23%	*	4%	= 100%
g.	Ronald Reagan	21%	41%	22%	14%	*	2%	= 100%
h.	Ted Kennedy	21%	43%	21%	10%	1%	4%	= 100%
i.	Ross Perot	6%	13%	5%	2%	47%	27%	= 100%
j.	Oprah Winfrey	22%	39%	8%	4%	12%	15%	= 100%
k.	Gary Hart	15%	57%	13%	4%	3%	8%	= 100%
l.	Jesse Jackson	13%	38%	24%	17%	2%	6%	= 100%
m.	Jesse Helms	3%	19%	15%	9%	26%	28%	= 100%
n.	Jane Fonda	11%	44%	21%	14%	2%	8%	= 100%
o.	George Bush	11%	56%	19%	7%	1%	6%	= 100%
p.	Jerry Falwell	4%	22%	26%	25%	10%	13%	= 100%
q.	Jimmy Carter	14%	56%	19%	8%	*	3%	= 100%
r.	Lee Iacocca	24%	42%	8%	5%	8%	13%	= 100%

*Less than 0.5 percent.

402. *(HAND RESPONDENT Card M)* Here are some other statements on a variety of topics. Please tell me how much you agree or disagree with each of these statements.

		COMPLETELY AGREE	MOSTLY AGREE	MOSTLY DISAGREE	COMPLETELY DISAGREE	DON'T KNOW	
a.	Prayer is an important part of my daily life	41%	35%	17%	6%	1%	= 100%
b.	We all will be called before God at the judgment day to answer for our sins	52%	29%	9%	5%	5%	= 100%
c.	Even today miracles are performed by the power of God	47%	35%	9%	4%	5%	= 100%
d.	I am sometimes very conscious of the presence of God	41%	39%	12%	4%	4%	= 100%
e.	I never doubt the existence of God	60%	28%	7%	3%	2%	= 100%
f.	School boards ought to have the right to fire teachers who are known homosexuals	27%	24%	28%	14%	7%	= 100%
g.	Books that contain dangerous ideas should be banned from public school libraries	24%	26%	25%	19%	6%	= 100%
h.	Nude magazines and X-rated movies provide harmless adult entertainment for those who enjoy it	14%	34%	26%	21%	5%	= 100%
i.	Freedom of speech should not extend to groups like the Communist Party or the Ku Klux Klan	16%	23%	36%	19%	6%	= 100%
j.	The police should be allowed to search the houses of known drug dealers without a court order	25%	26%	27%	18%	4%	= 100%
k.	Women should return to their traditional role in society	9%	21%	37%	29%	4%	= 100%
l.	Too many children are being raised in day care centers these days	23%	45%	22%	5%	5%	= 100%
m.	The government ought to be able to censor news stories that it feels threaten national security	19%	42%	21%	13%	5%	= 100%
n.	The news media should be free to report on any stories they feel are in the national interest	25%	49%	17%	5%	4%	= 100%
o.	AIDS might be God's punishment for immoral sexual behavior	17%	26%	22%	25%	10%	= 100%
p.	I have old-fashioned values about family and marriage	45%	42%	9%	2%	2%	= 100%
q.	There are clear guidelines about what's good or evil that apply to everyone regardless of their situation	34%	45%	12%	4%	5%	= 100%

		COMPLETELY AGREE	MOSTLY AGREE	MOSTLY DISAGREE	COMPLETELY DISAGREE	DON'T KNOW	
r.	Labor unions are necessary to protect the working person	19%	48%	21%	6%	6%	= 100%
s.	Labor unions have too much power	19%	40%	26%	7%	8%	= 100%
t.	Today it's really true that the rich just get richer while the poor get poorer	31%	43%	19%	3%	4%	= 100%
u.	I can usually tell whether I'll have a lot in common with someone by knowing how much education he or she has	5%	23%	49%	18%	5%	= 100%
v.	I don't have much in common with people of other races	3%	20%	54%	18%	5%	= 100%
w.	I often don't have enough money to make ends meet	14%	29%	44%	11%	2%	= 100%
x.	Money is one of my most important concerns	13%	34%	39%	12%	2%	= 100%
y.	I'm pretty well satisfied with the way things are going for me financially	11%	52%	27%	8%	2%	= 100%
z.	I feel it's my duty as a citizen to always vote	46%	39%	9%	3%	3%	= 100%
aa.	I'm interested in keeping up with national affairs	28%	53%	12%	3%	4%	= 100%
bb.	I'm generally bored by what goes on in Washington	8%	34%	41%	13%	4%	= 100%
cc.	I'm pretty interested in following *local* politics	16%	54%	22%	4%	4%	= 100%
dd.	Most issues discussed in Washington don't affect me personally	5%	26%	50%	15%	4%	= 100%
ee.	I feel guilty when I don't get a chance to vote	25%	41%	22%	6%	6%	= 100%
ff.	Sometimes I vote for a candidate without really knowing enough about him or her	9%	44%	28%	13%	6%	= 100%

NO QUESTIONS 403-499

500. *(HAND RESPONDENT Card N)* We are interested in how much each of these major events has affected your thinking about politics. While all of them are important events, we would like to know whether they shaped *your* views. As you think about your life, which *one* of these most affected your political views? *(INTERVIEWER: ACCEPT ONLY ONE RESPONSE. RECORD UNDER Q. 500.)*

		MOST	MOST AND SECOND MOST
a.	The Great Depression	12%	17%
b.	FDR and the New Deal	5%	8%
c.	World War II	7%	14%
d.	The Holocaust	3%	5%
e.	The McCarthy Era	1%	2%
f.	The Korean War	2%	4%
g.	The John F. Kennedy Presidency	9%	15%
h.	The Civil Rights Movement	7%	16%
i.	Assassinations of the 1960s—John and Robert Kennedy & Martin Luther King, Jr.	8%	18%
j.	The Vietnam War	19%	34%
k.	The Watergate Crisis	6%	17%
l.	The Jimmy Carter Presidency	3%	8%
m.	The Ronald Reagan Presidency	10%	20%
	DON'T KNOW	8%	8%
		100%	

(INTERVIEWER: RESPONDENT RETAINS Card N)

501. Which one was *second* most important in shaping your political views? *(RECORD ABOVE UNDER Q. 501.)*

502. *(HAND RESPONDENT Card O)* Here is a list of words and phrases people may use to describe candidates for President of the United States. Which *one* of these qualities would you most like to see in a candidate for President? *(CIRCLE ONE NUMBER UNDER Q. 502.)*

		Q. 502 MOST	MOST AND Q. 503 SECOND MOST
a.	Intelligent	10%	16%
b.	Caring	3%	5%
c.	Inspiring	1%	1%
d.	A strong leader	18%	33%
e.	Knowledgeable	5%	12%
f.	Decent	1%	3%
g.	Hard-working	1%	6%
h.	Exciting	*	*
i.	Gets things done	6%	14%
j.	Clear on issues	5%	11%
k.	Thoughtful	1%	1%
l.	Fair	1%	4%
m.	Good judgment in a crisis	19%	38%
n.	Decisive	1%	4%
o.	Likeable	*	1%
p.	Interesting personality	*	*
q.	Confident	1%	2%
r.	Religious	4%	7%
s.	Enthusiastic	*	1%
t.	Understands details	1%	2%
u.	Trustworthy	20%	34%
	Don't know	2%	2%
		100%	

*Less than 0.5 percent.

503. *(INTERVIEWER: RESPONDENT RETAINS Card O)* Which one is second most important to you? *(CIRCLE NUMBER UNDER Q. 503.)*

504. *(HAND RESPONDENT Card P)* For each of these areas of national interest, tell me if you think the Reagan Administration has *made progress* in solving problems, *tried but failed* to solve problems, *did not deal with* problems or *created* problems for the next president: *(READ LIST. CIRCLE ONE NUMBER FOR EACH ITEM.)*

		MADE PROGRESS	TRIED BUT FAILED	DID NOT DEAL WITH PROBLEM	CREATED PROBLEMS	DON'T KNOW	
a.	Foreign policy	34%	29%	6%	19%	12%	= 100%
b.	The budget deficit	13%	46%	11%	21%	9%	= 100%
c.	The trade imbalance	20%	33%	15%	15%	17%	= 100%
d.	Federal taxes	35%	25%	8%	20%	12%	= 100%
e.	Inflation	53%	20%	9%	11%	7%	= 100%
f.	Unemployment	43%	22%	17%	12%	6%	= 100%
g.	Interest rates	59%	13%	8%	9%	11%	= 100%
h.	Arms control	33%	30%	9%	16%	12%	= 100%
i.	The U.S. policy in Central America	13%	31%	5%	34%	17%	= 100%
j.	Race relations	25%	13%	40%	11%	11%	= 100%
k.	The gap between rich and poor	10%	19%	41%	20%	10%	= 100%
l.	Drug problems	42%	32%	14%	5%	7%	= 100%
m.	Public education	30%	20%	31%	9%	10%	= 100%
n.	Problems of farmers	12%	34%	27%	16%	11%	= 100%

505. In the long run, do you think the accomplishments of the Reagan Administration will outweigh its failures—or will the failures outweigh the accomplishments?
46% Accomplishments outweigh failures
41% Failures outweigh accomplishments
13% Don't know
100%

506. *(HAND RESPONDENT Card Q)* I'd like your opinion of some people and organizations. As I read from a list, please tell me which category on this card best describes your *overall* opinion of who or what I name. Probably, there will be some people and organizations on this list that you have never heard of. First, how would you describe your opinion of… *(READ ITEMS. CIRCLE ONE NUMBER FOR EACH ITEM.)*

		VERY FAVORABLE	MOSTLY FAVORABLE	MOSTLY UNFAVORABLE	VERY UNFAVORABLE	NEVER HEARD OF	CAN'T RATE	
a.	The Congress	10%	64%	16%	4%	*	6%	= 100%
b.	Franklin D. Roosevelt	32%	50%	6%	2%	1%	9%	= 100%
c.	Wall Street investors	5%	33%	30%	11%	2%	19%	= 100%
d.	John F. Kennedy	39%	47%	8%	3%	*	3%	= 100%
e.	Lawyers	7%	45%	30%	12%	1%	5%	= 100%
f.	The Supreme Court	13%	63%	15%	2%	*	7%	= 100%
g.	Mikhail Gorbachev	3%	37%	24%	14%	6%	16%	= 100%
h.	Martin Luther King, Jr.	29%	45%	14%	6%	*	6%	= 100%
i.	The CIA	5%	35%	35%	11%	*	14%	= 100%
j.	The nuclear freeze movement	16%	43%	18%	7%	2%	14%	= 100%
k.	Pope John Paul II	28%	48%	10%	4%	1%	9%	= 100%
l.	The daily newspaper you are most familiar with	22%	59%	12%	3%	*	4%	= 100%
m.	Network TV news	21%	63%	11%	3%	*	2%	= 100%
n.	The military	17%	63%	12%	4%	0%	4%	= 100%

*Less than 0.5 percent.

NO QUESTIONS 507-599

600. Some people seem to follow what's going on in government and public affairs most of the time, whether there's an election or not. Others aren't that interested. Would you say you follow what's going on in government and public affairs most of the time, some of the time, only now and then or hardly at all?

41% Most of the time
35% Some of the time
15% Only now and then
7% Hardly at all
2% Don't know
100%

601. In the election of *1980* when Jimmy Carter ran against Ronald Reagan, did things come up which kept you from voting or did you happen to vote? For whom?

31% Carter
33% Reagan
2% Other
2% Voted, don't remember for whom
30% Did *not* vote
2% Don't remember if voted
100%

602. In the election in November 1984, when Ronald Reagan ran against Walter Mondale, did things come up which kept you from voting or did you happen to vote? For whom?

40% Reagan
29% Mondale
2% Other
2% Voted, don't remember for whom
25% Did *not* vote
2% Don't remember if voted
100%

603. Is your name now recorded in the registration book of the voting precinct or election district where you now live? (That is, are you registered to vote?)

77% Yes—SKIP TO Q. 605
21% No—CONTINUE
1% Don't have to register } SKIP TO Q. 605
1% Don't know
100%

604. Do you plan to register so that you can vote in the next Presidential election? *(Based on those who are not currently registered)*

13% Yes
6% No
* Other
2% Don't know
21%

ASK EVERYONE:

605. If there is a primary election in your state next year, how likely is it that you will vote in either the Republican or Democratic primary for President? Is it very likely, somewhat likely, not too likely or not at all likely?

	REPUBLICAN AND REPUBLICAN LEANERS	**DEMOCRAT AND DEMOCRATIC LEANERS**
Very likely	65%	64%
Somewhat likely	18%	19%
Not too likely	7%	6%
Not at all likely	6%	6%
NO PRIMARY ELECTION (VOLUNTEERED)	1%	1%
Don't know	3%	4%
	100%	100%

*Less than 0.5 percent.

606. How often would you say you vote—always, nearly always, part of the time or seldom?

34% Always
37% Nearly always
11% Part of the time
6% Seldom
2% OTHER (SPECIFY): _____
9% Never vote *(VOLUNTEERED)* } GO TO Q. 609
1% Don't know
100%

607. Did you happen to vote in the Congressional elections that were held last November?

55% Yes
42% No
3% Don't know } SKIP TO Q. 609
100%

608. Was the U.S. Congressional candidate you voted for a Republican, a Democrat or did he/she belong to some other party? *(Based on those who voted in the Congressional Elections—55%)*

22% Republican
27% Democrat
1% Other
5% Don't know
55%

609. We would like to find out about some of the things people do to help a party or a candidate win an election. Which of the following things, if any, have you done in the *last four years* or so? *(READ LIST. CIRCLE ONE NUMBER FOR EACH ITEM.)*

		YES	**NO**	**DON'T KNOW**	
a.	Wore a campaign button, put a campaign sticker on your car or placed a sign in your window or in front of your house?	27%	71%	2%	= 100%
b.	Went to any political meetings, rallies, speeches or dinners in support of a particular candidate?	17%	81%	2%	= 100%
c.	Worked for a political party or a candidate running for office	11%	87%	2%	= 100%
d.	Checked-off the option on your federal income tax return applying one dollar of your taxes to the campaign fund?	30%	66%	4%	= 100%
e.	Contributed money to *an individual candidate* running for public office?	15%	83%	2%	= 100%
f.	Contributed money to a political party organization?	12%	86%	2%	= 100%
g.	Contributed money to *political action groups* such as groups sponsored by a union, or a business or any other issue groups that supported or opposed particular candidates in an election?	12%	86%	2%	= 100%

Now, just a few questions about your own reading, viewing and listening habits.

610. Some people are so busy that they don't get to read a newspaper every day. How about you—do you get a chance to read a newspaper just about every day or not?
66% Yes
33% No
  1% Don't know
100%

611. We're interested in how often people watch the major TV network evening news programs—by this we mean ABC World News Tonight with Peter Jennings, CBS Evening News with Dan Rather and NBC Nightly News with Tom Brokaw. Do you happen to watch network TV evening news programs *regularly* or not?
71% Yes—GO TO Q. 613
28% No
  1% Don't know
100%

612. Do you *sometimes* watch network TV evening news programs or do you *hardly ever* watch them? *(Based on those who do not regularly watch network TV evening news)*
16% Sometimes
10% Hardly ever
  2% Never *(VOLUNTEERED)*
  1% Don't know
29%

613. Which one of these do you rely on most for information on national affairs? *(READ)*
28% Your daily newspaper
56% Television
  2% Magazines
  9% Radio
  1% None *(VOLUNTEERED)*
  4% Don't know
100%

614. The following are actions people have taken in order to express their views on issues that concern them. For each, please tell me if you have done it *over the last four years* or so to express your view on any issue. *(READ LIST. CIRCLE ONE NUMBER FOR EACH ITEM.)*

		YES	NO	DON'T KNOW	
a.	Written a letter, telephoned or sent a telegram to an editor, public official or company	30%	69%	1%	= 100%
b.	Signed a petition	55%	43%	2%	= 100%
c.	Circulated a petition	10%	89%	1%	= 100%
d.	Voted for or against a candidate for public office only because of his or her position on *one* specific issue	27%	70%	3%	= 100%
e.	Attended a public hearing or a meeting of a special-interest organization	23%	76%	1%	= 100%
f.	Spoken at a public hearing or forum	6%	93%	1%	= 100%
g.	Boycotted a company	15%	84%	1%	= 100%
h.	Joined an organization in support of a particular cause	17%	81%	2%	= 100%
i.	Took part in a public demonstration	6%	93%	1%	= 100%
j.	Broke the law in a protest for a political or social cause	2%	97%	1%	= 100%
k.	Initiated or participated in a lawsuit	7%	92%	1%	= 100%
l.	Contacted your Representative to the U.S. House of Representatives	22%	77%	1%	= 100%
m.	Contacted your U.S. Senator	19%	79%	2%	= 100%

615. *(HAND RESPONDENT Card R)* For each statement please tell me whether you *completely* agree with it, *mostly* agree with it, mostly *disagree* with it or *completely* disagree with it. The first one is... *(CIRCLE ONE NUMBER FOR EACH ITEM.)*

		COMPLETELY AGREE	MOSTLY AGREE	MOSTLY DISAGREE	COMPLETELY DISAGREE	DON'T KNOW	
a.	I often don't become aware of political candidates until I see their advertising on television	10%	42%	34%	10%	4%	= 100%
b.	I get some sense of what a candidate is like through his or her TV commercials	7%	50%	31%	8%	4%	= 100%
c.	I like to have a picture of a candidate in my mind when I go to vote for him or her	16%	54%	16%	6%	8%	= 100%

We are interested in how people get to know about political candidates...

616. Which gives you a better idea of where a candidate stands on issues: news reports on TV or candidates' TV commercials?
   79% News reports
   13% Candidates' TV commercials
   __8%__ Don't know
   100%

617. Which gives you a better idea of what a candidate is like personally: news reports on TV or candidates' TV commercials?
   67% News reports
   24% Candidates' TV commercials
   __9%__ Don't know
   100%

618. *(HAND RESPONDENT Card S)* Which, if any, of these apply to you? Just call off all of the numbers for the items that apply to you. *(CHECK ALL THAT APPLY.)*
   44% Exercise regularly
   10% Belong to a health club
   24% Regularly participate in a sport
   51% Read for pleasure more than six books a year
   42% Enjoy rock and roll music
   49% Enjoy country and western music
   42% Enjoy classical music
   34% Watch Dallas, Dynasty, Knots Landing or Falcon Crest
   49% Watch Wheel of Fortune or other game shows
   60% Watch Family Ties or The Bill Cosby Show
   14% Read romance novels
   17% Go hunting
   34% Go camping
   26% Watch religious shows on TV
   14% Work with, lead or coach a youth group
   17% Belong to a fraternal or civic organization
   35% Regularly go out to dinner at formal restaurants
   15% Go to clubs or discos
   25% Attend theater, ballet, opera or classical music concerts
    9% Traveled overseas in the past year
    2% Belong to a country club
    2% None/DK

NO QUESTIONS 619-699